hamlyn

Golf Rules
ILLUSTRATED

2008
EDITION

Thirteenth edition
Compiled by R&A Rules Limited

D1354423

Contents

Foreword

This edition of *Golf Rules Illustrated* deals with the Rules of Golf that are effective from 1 January 2008. There have been a number of changes made in the most recent review of the Rules themselves, mainly aimed at simplifying and clarifying certain Rules that have caused difficulty in the recent past. These changes are incorporated in this edition.

Whereas the *Rule Book* itself is necessarily as concise as possible and designed to be carried easily in the pocket or golf bag, *Golf Rules Illustrated* is intended more as a reference document and companion to the *Rule Book*. It is designed to improve awareness and understanding of the Rules of Golf through the use of many photographs, drawings and descriptions of actual incidents in tournament golf.

This is the 13th edition of *Golf Rules Illustrated*. Its style and format continue to evolve, based on the feedback from golfers who have used earlier editions. We very much hope that you will enjoy and benefit from this new edition.

ALAN W. J. HOLMES
Chairman, Rules of Golf Committee,
R&A Rules Limited

R&A Rules Limited
With effect from 1 January 2004, the responsibilities and authority of The Royal and Ancient Golf Club of St Andrews in making, interpreting and giving decisions of the Rules of Golf were transferred to R&A Rules Limited.

Gender
In the Rules of Golf, the gender used in relation to any person is understood to include both genders.

Golfers with Disabilities
The R&A publication entitled *A Modification of the Rules of Golf for Golfers with Disabilities* contains permissible modifications of the Rules of Golf to accommodate disabled golfers; it is available through The R&A.

PRINCIPAL CHANGES INTRODUCED IN THE 2008 CODE

General

The changes to the Rules generally fall into two broad categories: (1) those that improve the clarity of the Rules and (2) those that reduce the penalties in certain circumstances to ensure that they are proportionate.

Definitions

Advice

Amended to allow the exchange of information on distance, as it is not considered to be "advice".

Lost Ball

Amended to clarify substituted ball issues and to include the concept of "stroke-and-distance" (see corresponding changes to Rules 18-1, 24-3, 25-1c, 26 and 27-1).

Matches

Definition withdrawn and replaced by the two new Definitions, "Forms of Match Play" and "Forms of Stroke Play".

Rules

Rule 1-2. Exerting Influence on Ball

Note added to clarify what constitutes a serious breach of Rule 1-2.

Rule 4-1. Form and Make of Clubs

Amended to reduce the penalty for carrying, but not using, a non-conforming club or a club in breach of Rule 4-2, from disqualification to the same as carrying more than 14 clubs.

Rule 12-1. Searching for Ball; Seeing Ball

Amended to include searching for a ball in an obstruction.

Rule 12-2. Identifying Ball

Amended to allow a player to lift his ball for identification in a hazard (see corresponding change to Rule 15-3, removing the exemption from penalty for playing a wrong ball in a hazard).

Rule 13-4. Ball in Hazard; Prohibited Actions

Exception 1 amended for clarification; Exception 2 amended to refer to Rule 13-2 and to eliminate the reference to assistance in the player's subsequent play of the hole; Exception 3 added to exempt a player from penalty under Rule 13-4a (testing the condition of the hazard) in certain circumstances.

Rule 14-3. Artificial Devices, Unusual Equipment and Unusual Use of Equipment

Amended to refer to the unusual use of equipment (see also new Exception on use of equipment in a traditionally accepted manner) and new Exception added for players with a legitimate medical reason to use an artificial device or unusual equipment. Note added to clarify that a Local Rule may be introduced allowing the use of distance measuring devices; previously authorised by Decision only.

Rule 15-2. Substituted Ball

Exception added to avoid a "double penalty" when player incorrectly substitutes ball and plays from the wrong place (see corresponding change to Rule 20-7c).

Rules 15-3. Wrong Ball

Amended to remove the exemption from penalty for playing a wrong ball in a hazard (see corresponding change to Rule 12-2, allowing a player to lift a ball for identification in a hazard).

Rule 16-1e. Standing Astride or on Line of Putt

Exception added to apply no penalty if act was inadvertent or to avoid standing on another player's line of putt; previously authorised by Decision only.

Rule 18. Ball at Rest Moved

Penalty statement amended to avoid a "double penalty" when a player lifts his ball without authority and incorrectly substitutes ball (see related changes to Rules 15-2 and 20-7c).

Rule 18-1. Ball at Rest Moved; by Outside Agency

Note added to clarify procedure when ball might have been moved by an outside agency.

Rule 19-2. Ball in Motion Deflected or Stopped by Player, Partner, Caddie or Equipment

Amended to reduce the penalty in both match play and stroke play to one stroke.

Rule 20-3a. Placing and Replacing; By Whom and Where

Amended to reduce the penalty for having the wrong person place or replace a ball to one stroke.

Rule 20-7c. Playing from Wrong Place; Stroke Play

Note added to avoid a "double penalty" when player plays from the wrong place and incorrectly substitutes ball (see corresponding change to Rule 15-2).

Rule 24-1. Movable Obstruction

Amended to allow a flagstick, whether attended, removed or held up, to be moved when a ball is in motion.

Rule 24-3. Ball in Obstruction Not Found;
Rule 25-1c. Ball in Abnormal Ground Condition Not Found;
Rule 26. Water Hazards (including Lateral Water Hazards);
Rule 27-1. Stroke and Distance, Ball Out of Bounds; Ball Not Found Within Five Minutes

In the above Rules, the term "reasonable evidence" has been replaced by "known or virtually certain" when determining whether a ball that has not been found may be treated as in an obstruction (Rule 24-3), an abnormal ground condition (Rule 25-1) or a water hazard (Rule 26-1). See corresponding changes to Definition of Lost Ball and Rule 18-1.

Appendix I

Seams of Cut Turf

New specimen Local Rule added.

Temporary Immovable Obstructions

Clause II of the specimen Local Rule amended to include an additional requirement that, for intervention relief to be granted, the temporary immovable obstruction must be on the player's line of play.

Appendix II

Adjustability

Amended to allow forms of adjustability other than weight adjustment, subject to evaluation by The R&A.

Clubhead; Plain in Shape

Amended to clarify meaning of "plain in shape" and list some of the features that are not permitted; previously detailed in guidelines on equipment Rules.

Clubhead; Dimensions, Volume and Moment of Inertia

Sections added on moment of inertia and putter head dimensions; previously detailed in guidelines on equipment Rules and test protocols.

Clubhead; Spring Effect and Dynamic Properties

New section added on spring effect. The limit, as detailed in the Pendulum Test Protocol, now applies to all clubs (except putters) and in all forms of the game; previously covered by condition of competition.

HOW TO USE THE RULE BOOK

It is understood that not everyone who has a copy of the Rules of Golf will read it from cover to cover. Most golfers only consult the Rule book when they have a Rules issue on the course that needs to be resolved. However, to ensure that you have a basic understanding of the Rules and that you play golf in a reasonable manner, it is recommended that you at least read the Quick Guide to the Rules of Golf and the Etiquette Section contained within this publication.

The following points will assist you in using the Rule book efficiently and accurately:

Understand the Words

The Rule book is written in a very precise and deliberate fashion. You should be aware of and understand the following differences in word use:

- "may" (e.g. the player may cancel the stroke) means the action is optional
- "should" (e.g. the marker should check the score) means the action is recommended but is not mandatory
- "must" (e.g. the player's clubs must conform) means it is an instruction and there is a penalty if it is not carried out
- "a ball" (e.g drop a ball behind the point) means you may substitute another ball (e.g. Rules 26, 27 and 28)
- "the ball" (e.g. the player must lift the ball and drop it) means you must not substitute another ball (e.g. Rules 24-2 and 25-1)

Know the Definitions

There are over fifty defined terms (e.g. abnormal ground condition, through the green, etc) and these form the foundation around which the Rules of Play are written. A good knowledge of the defined terms (which are italicised throughout the book) is very important to the correct application of the Rules.

The Facts of the Case

To answer any question on the Rules you must consider the facts of the case in some detail. You should identify:

- The form of play (e.g. match play or stroke play, single, foursome or four-ball)
- Who is involved (e.g. the player, his partner or caddie, an outside agency)
- Where the incident occurred (e.g. on the teeing ground, in a bunker or water hazard, on the putting green)
- What actually happened
- The timing of the incident (e.g. has the player now returned his score card, has the competition closed)

Refer to the Book

If in doubt on any of the Rules, play the course as you find it and play the ball as it lies. On returning to the Clubhouse, you can refer the matter to the Committee and it may be that reference to the "Decisions on the Rules of Golf" will assist in resolving any queries that are not entirely clear from the Rule book itself.

A QUICK GUIDE TO THE RULES OF GOLF

As golf is a self-regulating game, all golfers should have a good understanding of the fundamental Rules, as contained in this guide. However, this guide is not a substitute for the Rules of Golf, which should be consulted whenever any doubt arises. For more information on the points covered in this guide, please refer to the relevant Rule.

General Points

Before commencing your round:
- Read the Local Rules on the score card or the notice board.
- Put an identification mark on your ball. Many golfers play the same brand and model of ball and if you can't identify your ball, it is considered lost. (Rules 12-2 and 27-1)
- Count your clubs. You are allowed a maximum of 14 clubs. (Rule 4-4)

During the round:
- Don't ask for "advice" from anyone except your partner (i.e. a player on your side) or your caddies. Don't give advice to anyone except your partner. You may ask for information on the Rules, distances and the position of hazards, the flagstick, etc. (Rule 8-1)
- Don't play any practice shots during play of a hole. (Rule 7-2)

At the end of your round:
- In match play, ensure the result of the match is posted.
- In stroke play, ensure that your score card is completed properly and return it as soon as possible. (Rule 6-6)

The Rules of Play

Tee Shot (**Rule 11**)
Play your tee shot from between, and not in front of, the tee-markers.

You may play your tee shot from up to two club-lengths behind the front line of the tee-markers.

If you play your tee shot from outside this area, in match play there is no penalty, but your opponent may require you to replay your stroke; in stroke play you incur a two-stroke penalty and must correct the error by playing from within the correct area.

Playing the Ball (**Rules 12, 13, 14 and 15**)
If you think a ball is yours but cannot see your identification mark, with the permission of your marker or opponent, you may mark and lift the ball to identify it. (Rule 12-2)

Play the ball as it lies. Don't improve your lie, the area of your intended stance or swing, or your line of play by moving, bending or breaking anything fixed or growing, except in fairly taking your stance or making your swing. Don't improve your lie by pressing anything down. (Rule 13-2)

If your ball is in a bunker or a water hazard, don't touch the ground in either type of hazard, or touch water in the water hazard, with your hand or club before your downswing and don't move loose impediments. (Rule 13-4)

You must swing the club and make a stroke at the ball. It is not permissible to push, scrape or spoon the ball. (Rule 14-1)

If you play a wrong ball, in match play you lose the hole; in stroke play you incur a two-stroke penalty and you must then correct the mistake by playing the correct ball. (Rule 15-3)

On the Putting Green (**Rules 16 and 17**)
You may mark, lift and clean your ball on the putting green; always replace it on the exact spot. (Rule 16-1b)

You may repair ball marks and old hole plugs, but not any other damage, such as spike marks. (Rule 16-1c)

When making a stroke on the putting green, you should ensure that the flagstick is removed or attended. The flagstick may also be removed or attended when the ball lies off the putting green. (Rule 17)

Ball at Rest Moved (Rule 18)

Generally, when the ball is in play, if you accidentally cause your ball to move, lift it when not permitted or it moves after you have addressed it, add a penalty stroke and replace your ball. However, see the exceptions under Rule 18-2a. (Rule 18-2)

If someone else moves your ball at rest or it is moved by another ball, replace it without penalty to you.

Ball in Motion Deflected or Stopped (Rule 19)

If a ball struck by you is deflected or stopped by you, your partner, your caddie or your equipment, add a penalty stroke and the ball is played as it lies. (Rule 19-2)

If a ball struck by you is deflected or stopped by another ball at rest, there is no penalty and the ball is played as it lies, except in stroke play where you incur a two-stroke penalty if your ball and the other ball were on the putting green before you played. (Rule 19-5a)

Lifting, Dropping and Placing the Ball (Rule 20)

Before lifting a ball that has to be replaced (e.g. when the ball is lifted on the putting green to clean it), the position of the ball must be marked. (Rule 20-1)

When the ball is being lifted in order to drop or place it in another position (e.g. dropping within two club-lengths under the unplayable ball Rule), it is not mandatory to mark its position although it is recommended that you do so.

When dropping, stand upright, hold the ball at shoulder height and arm's length and drop it. A dropped ball must be re-dropped if it rolls to a position where there is interference from the condition from which free relief is being taken (e.g. an immovable obstruction), if it comes to rest more than two club-lengths from where it was dropped, or if it comes to rest nearer the

hole than its original position, the nearest point of relief or where the ball last crossed the margin of a water hazard.

There are nine situations in total when a dropped ball must be re-dropped and they are covered in Rule 20-2c.

If a ball dropped for a second time rolls into any of these positions, place it where it first struck the course when re-dropped. (Rule 20-2c)

Ball Assisting or Interfering with Play (Rule 22)

You may lift your ball or have any other ball lifted if you think the ball might assist another player.

You must not agree to leave a ball in position in order to assist another player.
You may have any ball lifted if it might interfere with your play.

A ball that is lifted due to it assisting or interfering with play must not be cleaned, unless it is lifted from the putting green.

Loose Impediments (Rule 23)

You may move a loose impediment (i.e. natural loose objects such as stones, detached leaves and twigs) unless the loose impediment and your ball are in the same hazard. If you remove a loose impediment and this causes your ball to move, the ball must be replaced and (unless your ball was on the putting green) you incur a one-stroke penalty. (Rule 23-1)

Movable Obstructions (Rule 24)

Movable obstructions (i.e. artificial movable objects such as rakes, tin cans, etc.) located anywhere may be moved without penalty. If the ball moves as a result, it must be replaced without penalty.

If a ball is on a movable obstruction, the ball may be lifted, the obstruction removed and the ball dropped, without penalty, on the spot directly under where the ball lay on the obstruction, except that on the putting green, the ball is placed on that spot.

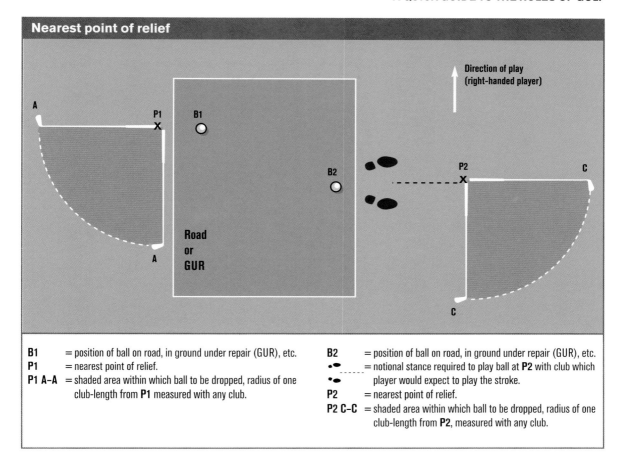

Nearest point of relief

B1	= position of ball on road, in ground under repair (GUR), etc.
P1	= nearest point of relief.
P1 A–A	= shaded area within which ball to be dropped, radius of one club-length from **P1** measured with any club.

B2	= position of ball on road, in ground under repair (GUR), etc.
•● ------	= notional stance required to play ball at **P2** with club which
•●	player would expect to play the stroke.
P2	= nearest point of relief.
P2 C–C	= shaded area within which ball to be dropped, radius of one club-length from **P2**, measured with any club.

Immovable Obstructions and Abnormal Ground Conditions (Rules 24-2 and 25-1)

An immovable obstruction is an artificial immovable object such as a building or an artificially-surfaced road (but check the Local Rules for the status of roads and paths). An abnormal ground condition is either casual water, ground under repair or a hole, cast or runway made by a burrowing animal, a reptile or a bird.

Except when the ball is in a water hazard, free relief is available from immovable obstructions and abnormal ground conditions when the condition physically interferes with the lie of the ball, your stance or your swing. You may lift the ball and drop it within one club-length of the "nearest point of relief" (see Definition of "Nearest Point of Relief"), but not nearer the hole than the nearest point of relief (see diagram above).

If the ball is on the putting green, it is placed at the nearest point of relief.

There is no relief for intervention on your line of play unless both your ball and the condition are on the putting green.

As an additional option when the ball is in a bunker, you may take relief from the condition behind the bunker under penalty of one stroke. The above diagram illustrates the term "nearest point of relief" in Rules 24-2 and 25-1 in the case of a right-handed player.

Water Hazards (Rule 26)

If your ball is in a water hazard (yellow stakes and/or lines) you may play the ball as it lies or, under penalty of one stroke:

- play a ball from where you hit the ball into the hazard, or
- drop any distance behind the water hazard keeping a straight line between the hole, the

point where the ball last crossed the margin of the water hazard and the spot on which the ball is dropped.

If your ball is in a lateral water hazard (red stakes and/or lines), in addition to the options for a ball in a water hazard (see above), under penalty of one stroke, you may drop within two club-lengths of, and not nearer the hole than:

- the point where the ball last crossed the margin of the hazard, or
- a point on the opposite side of the hazard equidistant to the hole from the point where the ball last crossed the margin.

Ball Lost or Out of Bounds; Provisional Ball (Rule 27)

Check the Local Rules on the score card to identify the boundaries of the course.

If your ball is lost outside a water hazard or out of bounds you must play another ball from the spot where the last shot was played, under penalty of one stroke, i.e. stroke and distance.

You are allowed 5 minutes to search for a ball, after which, if it is not found or identified, it is lost.

If, after playing a shot, you think your ball may be lost outside a water hazard or out of bounds you should play a 'provisional ball'. You must state that it is a provisional ball and play it before you go forward to search for the original ball.

If it transpires that the original ball is lost (other than in a water hazard) or out of bounds, you must continue with the provisional ball, under penalty of one stroke. If the original ball is found in bounds, you must continue play of the hole with it, and must stop play with the provisional ball.

Ball Unplayable (see Rule 28)

If your ball is in a water hazard, the unplayable ball Rule does not apply and you must proceed under the water hazard Rule if taking relief. Elsewhere on the course, if you believe your ball is unplayable, you may under penalty of one stroke:

- play a ball from where the last shot was played, or
- drop a ball any distance behind the point where the ball lay keeping a straight line between the hole, the point where the ball lay and the spot on which the ball is dropped, or
- drop a ball within two club-lengths of where the ball lies not nearer the hole.

If your ball is in a bunker you may proceed as above, except that if you are dropping back on a line or within two club-lengths, you must drop in the bunker.

Etiquette

If you have not already done so, you should also read the Etiquette Section – not more Rules as such, but a practical guide to getting around the course safely, in good time, with consideration for others and having taken good care of the course.

SECTION 1
ETIQUETTE; BEHAVIOUR ON THE COURSE

Introduction
This section provides guidelines on the manner in which the game of golf should be played. If they are followed, all players will gain maximum enjoyment from the game. The overriding principle is that consideration should be shown to others on the course at all times.

The Spirit of the Game
Golf is played, for the most part, without the supervision of a referee or umpire. The game relies on the integrity of the individual to show consideration for other players and to abide by the Rules. All players should conduct themselves in a disciplined manner, demonstrating courtesy and sportsmanship at all times, irrespective of how competitive they may be. This is the spirit of the game of golf.

Safety
Players should ensure that no one is standing close by or in a position to be hit by the club, the ball or any stones, pebbles, twigs or the like when they make a stroke or practice swing.

Players should not play until the players in front are out of range.

Players should always alert greenstaff nearby or ahead when they are about to make a stroke that might endanger them.

If a player plays a ball in a direction where there is a danger of hitting someone, he should immediately shout a warning. The traditional word of warning in such situations is "fore".

Consideration for Other Players
No Disturbance or Distraction Players should always show consideration for other players on the course and should not disturb their play by moving, talking or making unnecessary noise.

Players should ensure that any electronic device taken onto the course does not distract other players.

On the teeing ground, a player should not tee his ball until it is his turn to play.

Players should not stand close to or directly behind the ball, or directly behind the hole, when a player is about to play.

On the Putting Green On the putting green, players should not stand on another player's line of putt or, when he is making a stroke, cast a shadow over his line of putt.

Players should remain on or close to the putting green until all other players in the group have holed out.

Scoring In stroke play, a player who is acting as a marker should, if necessary, on the way to the next tee, check the score with the player concerned and record it.

Players should be ready to play as soon as it is their turn. This can be achieved by lining up putts while other players are playing, provided there is no disturbance or distraction for them. Here Phil Mickelson putts out while Tiger Woods prepares for his putt.

Pace of Play

Play at Good Pace and Keep Up Players should play at a good pace. The Committee may establish pace of play guidelines that all players should follow.

It is a group's responsibility to keep up with the group in front. If it loses a clear hole and it is delaying the group behind, it should invite the group behind to play through, irrespective of the number of players in that group. Where a group has not lost a clear hole, but it is apparent that the group behind can play faster, it should invite the faster moving group to play through.

Be Ready to Play Players should be ready to play as soon as it is their turn to play. When playing on or near the putting green, they should leave their bags or carts in such a position as will enable quick movement off the green and towards the next tee. When the play of a hole has been completed, players should immediately leave the putting green.

Lost Ball If a player believes his ball may be lost outside a water hazard or is out of bounds, to save time, he should play a provisional ball.

Players searching for a ball should signal the players in the group behind them to play through as soon as it becomes apparent that the ball will not easily be found. They should not search for five minutes before doing so. Having allowed the group behind to play through, they should not continue play until that group has passed and is out of range.

Priority on the Course

Unless otherwise determined by the Committee, priority on the course is determined by a group's pace of play. Any group playing a whole round is entitled to pass a group playing a shorter round. The term 'group' includes a single player.

Care of the Course

Bunkers Before leaving a bunker, players should carefully fill up and smooth over all

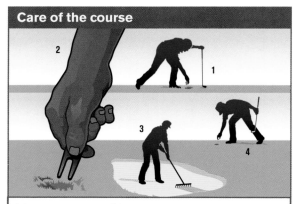

Care of the course

(1) Always repair divots, (2) carefully repair pitch marks on the putting green and (3) smooth over footprints and other marks when leaving a bunker. (4) Do not lean on your putter when removing the ball from the hole.

holes and footprints made by them and any nearby made by others. If a rake is within reasonable proximity of the bunker, the rake should be used for this purpose.

Repair of Divots, Ball-Marks and Damage by Shoes Players should carefully repair any divot holes made by them and any damage to the putting green made by the impact of a ball (whether or not made by the player himself). On completion of the hole by all players in the group, damage to the putting green caused by golf shoes should be repaired.

Preventing Unnecessary Damage Players should avoid causing damage to the course by removing divots when taking practice swings or by hitting the head of a club into the ground, whether in anger or for any other reason.

Players should ensure that no damage is done to the putting green when putting down bags or the flagstick.

In order to avoid damaging the hole, players and caddies should not stand too close to the hole and should take care during the handling of the flagstick and the removal of a ball from the hole. The head of a club should not be used to remove a ball from the hole.

Players should not lean on their clubs when on the putting green, particularly when removing the ball from the hole.

The flagstick should be properly replaced in the hole before the players leave the putting green.

Local notices regulating the movement of golf carts should be strictly observed.

Conclusion; Penalties for Breach

If players follow the guidelines in this section, it will make the game more enjoyable for everyone.

If a player consistently disregards these guidelines during a round or over a period of time to the detriment of others, it is recommended that the Committee considers taking appropriate disciplinary action against the offending player. Such action may, for example, include prohibiting play for a limited time on the course or in a certain number of competitions. This is considered to be justifiable in terms of protecting the interests of the majority of golfers who wish to play in accordance with these guidelines.

In the case of a serious breach of etiquette, the Committee may disqualify a player under Rule 33-7.

FAQ

Q Does a single player have any standing on the golf course?

A Different players play at different speeds, and whilst players should not have to run round the course, players should be aware of the fact that there are other players on the course at the same time and they should, therefore, act with common sense and courtesy towards those other players.

The Etiquette section suggests that, unless otherwise determined by the Committee, priority on the course is determined by a group's pace of play, and the term "group" includes a single player. The Pace of Play part of the Etiquette section also states that, "It is a group's responsibility to keep up with the group in front. If it loses a clear hole and it is delaying the group behind, it should invite the group behind to play through, irrespective of the number of players in that group. Where a group has not lost a clear hole, but it is apparent that the group behind can play faster, it should invite the faster moving group to play through." Therefore, a slow group should give way, where possible, to a faster group, and single golfers should have the same rights as all other players.

SECTION 2
DEFINITIONS

The Definitions are listed alphabetically and, in the *Rules* themselves, defined terms are in *italics*.

Abnormal Ground Conditions An "*abnormal ground condition*" is any *casual water*, *ground under repair* or hole, cast or runway on the *course* made by a *burrowing animal*, a reptile or a bird.

Addressing the Ball A player has "*addressed the ball*" when he has taken his *stance* and has also grounded his club, except that in a *hazard* a

player has *addressed the ball* when he has taken his *stance*.

Advice "*Advice*" is any counsel or suggestion that could influence a player in determining his play, the choice of a club or the method of making a *stroke*.

Information on the *Rules*, distance or matters of public information, such as the position of *hazards* or the *flagstick* on the *putting green*, is not *advice*.

Ball Deemed to Move See "*Move or Moved*".

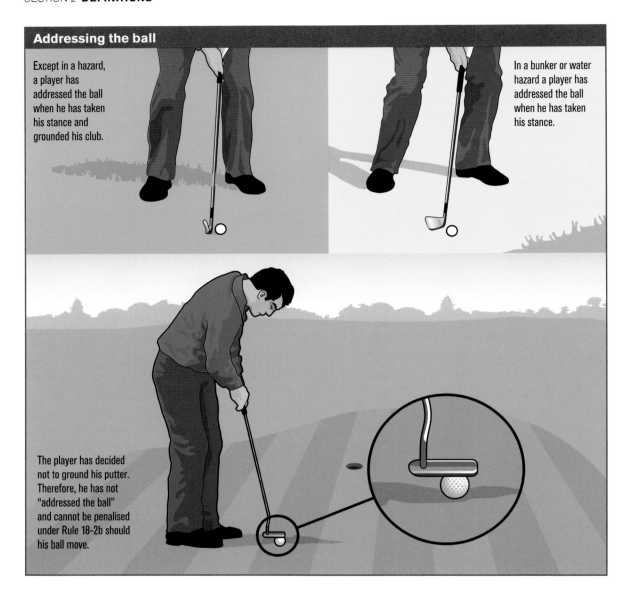

Addressing the ball

Except in a hazard, a player has addressed the ball when he has taken his stance and grounded his club.

In a bunker or water hazard a player has addressed the ball when he has taken his stance.

The player has decided not to ground his putter. Therefore, he has not "addressed the ball" and cannot be penalised under Rule 18-2b should his ball move.

Ball Holed See "*Holed*".

Ball Lost See "*Lost Ball*".

Ball in Play A ball is "*in play*" as soon as the player has made a *stroke* on the *teeing ground*. It remains *in play* until it is *holed*, except when it is *lost*, *out of bounds* or lifted, or another ball has been *substituted* whether or not the substitution is permitted; a ball so *substituted* becomes the *ball in play*.

If a ball is played from outside the *teeing ground* when the player is starting play of a hole, or when attempting to correct this mistake, the ball is not *in play* and Rule 11-4 or 11-5 applies. Otherwise, *ball in play* includes a ball played from outside the *teeing ground* when the player elects or is required to play his next *stroke* from the *teeing ground*.

Exception in match play: *Ball in play* includes a ball played by the player from outside the *teeing ground* when starting play of a hole if the opponent does not require the *stroke* to be cancelled in accordance with Rule 11-4a.

Bunker

Tim Clarke plays out of one of the bunkers at Royal Liverpool at the 2006 Open Championship. A bunker face consisting of stacked turf, whether grass covered or earthen, is not part of the bunker.

Best-Ball See "*Forms of Match Play*".

Bunker A "*bunker*" is a *hazard* consisting of a prepared area of ground, often a hollow, from which turf or soil has been removed and replaced with sand or the like.

Grass-covered ground bordering or within a *bunker* including a stacked turf face (whether grass-covered or earthen), is not part of the *bunker*.

A wall or lip of the *bunker* not covered with grass is part of the *bunker*. The margin of a *bunker* extends vertically downwards, but not upwards.

A ball is in a *bunker* when it lies in or any part of it touches the *bunker*.

Burrowing Animal A "*burrowing animal*" is an animal (other than a worm, insect or the like) that makes a hole for habitation or shelter, such as a rabbit, mole, groundhog, gopher or salamander.

Note: A hole made by a non-burrowing animal, such as a dog, is not an *abnormal ground condition* unless marked or declared as *ground under repair*.

Caddie A "*caddie*" is one who assists the player in accordance with the *Rules*, which may include carrying or handling the player's clubs during play.

When one *caddie* is employed by more than one player, he is always deemed to be the *caddie* of the player sharing the *caddie* whose ball (or whose *partner's* ball) is involved, and *equipment* carried by him is deemed to be that player's *equipment*, except when the *caddie* acts upon

Caddie

A caddie will carry a player's clubs and offer advice on club selection, the direction of play and line for putting.

Casual water

Casual water is an 'abnormal ground condition' and a player may take relief from such a condition under Rule 25-1.

specific directions of another player (or the *partner* of another player) sharing the *caddie*, in which case he is considered to be that other player's *caddie*.

Casual Water "*Casual water*" is any temporary accumulation of water on the *course* that is not in a *water hazard* and is visible before or after the player takes his *stance*. Snow and natural ice, other than frost, are either *casual water* or *loose impediments*, at the option of the player. Manufactured ice is an *obstruction*. Dew and frost are not *casual water*.

A ball is in *casual water* when it lies in or any part of it touches the *casual water*.

Committee The "*Committee*" is the committee in charge of the competition or, if the matter does not arise in a competition, the committee in charge of the *course*.

Competitor A "*competitor*" is a player in a stroke play competition. A "*fellow-competitor*" is any person with whom the *competitor* plays. Neither is *partner* of the other.

In stroke play *foursome* and *four-ball* competitions, where the context so admits, the word "*competitor*" or "*fellow-competitor*" includes his *partner*.

Course The "*course*" is the whole area within any boundaries established by the *Committee* (see Rule 33-2).

Equipment "*Equipment*" is anything used, worn or carried by the player or anything carried for the player by his *partner* or either of their *caddies*, except any ball he has played at the hole being played and any small object, such as a coin or a *tee*, when used to mark the position of a ball or the extent of an area in which a ball is to be dropped. *Equipment* includes a golf cart, whether or not motorised.

Note 1: A ball played at the hole being played is *equipment* when it has been lifted and not put back into play.

Note 2: When a golf cart is shared by two or more players, the cart and everything in it are deemed to be the *equipment* of one of the players sharing the cart.

If the cart is being moved by one of the players (or the *partner* of one of the players) sharing it, the cart and everything in it are deemed to be that player's *equipment*.

Otherwise, the cart and everything in it are deemed to be the *equipment* of the player

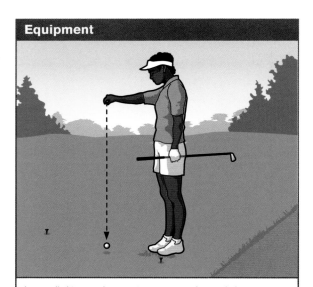

Equipment

Any small object, such as a coin or a tee, used to mark the extent of an area in which a ball can be dropped is not equipment of the player.

sharing the cart whose ball (or whose *partner's* ball) is involved.

Fellow-Competitor See "*Competitor*".

Flagstick The "*flagstick*" is a movable straight indicator, with or without bunting or other material attached, centered in the *hole* to show its position. It must be circular in cross-section. Padding or shock absorbent material that might unduly influence the movement of the ball is prohibited.

Forecaddie A "*forecaddie*" is one who is employed by the *Committee* to indicate to players the position of balls during play. He is an *outside agency*.

Forms of Match Play
Single: A match in which one player plays against another player.
Threesome: A match in which one player plays against two other players, and each *side* plays one ball.

Foursome: A match in which two players play against two other players, and each *side* plays one ball.
Three-Ball: Three players play a match against one another, each playing his own ball. Each player is playing two distinct matches.
Best-Ball: A match in which one player plays against the better ball of two other players or the best ball of three other players.
Four-Ball: A match in which two players play their better ball against the better ball of two other players.

Forms of Stroke Play
Individual: A competition in which each *competitor* plays as an individual.
Foursome: A competition in which two *competitors* play as *partners* and play one ball.
Four-Ball: A competition in which two *competitors* play as *partners*, each playing his own ball. The lower score of the *partners* is the score for the hole. If one *partner* fails to complete the play of a hole, there is no penalty.

Ground under repair

May I take a free drop from this pile of grass cuttings?

No. They have obviously been thrown under that bush to rot away. They are not piled for removal nor are they marked as ground under repair.

Note: For bogey, par and Stableford competitions, see Rule 32-1.

Four-Ball See "*Forms of Match Play*" and "*Forms of Stroke Play*".

Foursome See "*Forms of Match Play*" and *Forms of Stroke Play*".

Ground Under Repair "*Ground under repair*" is any part of the *course* so marked by order of the *Committee* or so declared by its authorised representative. All ground and any grass, bush, tree or other growing thing within the *ground under repair* are part of the *ground under repair*. *Ground under repair* includes material piled for removal and a hole made by a greenkeeper, even if not so marked. Grass cuttings and other material left on the *course* that have been abandoned and are not intended to be removed are not *ground under repair* unless so marked.

When the margin of *ground under repair* is defined by stakes, the stakes are inside the *ground under repair*, and the margin of the *ground under repair* is defined by the nearest outside points of the stakes at ground level. When both stakes and lines are used to indicate *ground under repair*, the stakes identify the *ground under repair* and the lines define the margin of the *ground under repair*. When the margin of *ground under repair* is defined by a line on the ground, the line itself is in the *ground under repair*. The margin of *ground under repair* extends vertically downwards but not upwards.

A ball is in *ground under repair* when it lies in or any part of it touches the *ground under repair*.

Stakes used to define the margin of or identify *ground under repair* are *obstructions*.

Note: The *Committee* may make a Local Rule prohibiting play from *ground under repair* or an environmentally-sensitive area defined as *ground under repair*.

Hazards A "*hazard*" is any *bunker* or *water hazard*.

Hole The "*hole*" must be 4¼ inches (108 mm) in diameter and at least 4 inches (101.6 mm) deep. If a lining is used, it must be sunk at least 1 inch (25.4 mm) below the *putting green* surface unless the nature of the soil makes it impracticable to do so; its outer diameter must not exceed 4¼ inches (108 mm).

Holed A ball is "*holed*" when it is at rest within the circumference of the *hole* and all of it is below the level of the lip of the *hole*.

Honour The player who is to play first from the *teeing ground* is said to have the "*honour*".

Lateral Water Hazard A "*lateral water hazard*" is a *water hazard* or that part of a *water hazard* so situated that it is not possible, or is deemed by the *Committee* to be impracticable, to drop a ball behind the *water hazard* in accordance with Rule 26-1b. All ground and water within the margin of a *lateral water hazard* are part of the *lateral water hazard*.

When the margin of a *lateral water hazard* is defined by stakes, the stakes are inside the *lateral water hazard*, and the margin of the *hazard* is defined by the nearest outside points of the stakes at ground level. When both stakes and lines are used to indicate a *lateral water hazard*, the stakes identify the *hazard* and the lines define the *hazard* margin. When the margin of a *lateral water hazard* is defined by a line on the ground, the line itself is in the *lateral water hazard*. The margin of a *lateral water hazard* extends vertically upwards and downwards.

A ball is in a *lateral water hazard* when it lies in or any part of it touches the *lateral water hazard*.

Stakes used to define the margin of or identify a *lateral water hazard* are *obstructions*.

Note 1: That part of a *water hazard* to be played as a *lateral water hazard* must be distinctively marked. Stakes or lines used to define the margin of or identify a *lateral water hazard* must be red.

Note 2: The *Committee* may make a Local Rule prohibiting play from an environmentally-sensitive area defined as a *lateral water hazard*.

Note 3: The *Committee* may define a *lateral water hazard* as a *water hazard*.

Line of Play The "*line of play*" is the direction that the player wishes his ball to take after a *stroke*, plus a reasonable distance on either side of the intended direction. The *line of play* extends vertically upwards from the ground, but does not extend beyond the *hole*.

Line of Putt The "*line of putt*" is the line that the player wishes his ball to take after a *stroke* on the *putting green*. Except with respect to Rule 16-1e, the *line of putt* includes a reasonable distance on either side of the intended line. The *line of putt* does not extend beyond the *hole*.

Loose Impediments "*Loose impediments*" are natural objects, including:
- stones, leaves, twigs, branches and the like,
- dung, and
- worms, insects and the like, and the casts and heaps made by them,

provided they are not:
- fixed or growing,
- solidly embedded, or
- adhering to the ball.

Sand and loose soil are *loose impediments* on the *putting green*, but not elsewhere.

Snow and natural ice, other than frost, are either *casual water* or *loose impediments* at the option of the player.

Dew and frost are not *loose impediments*.

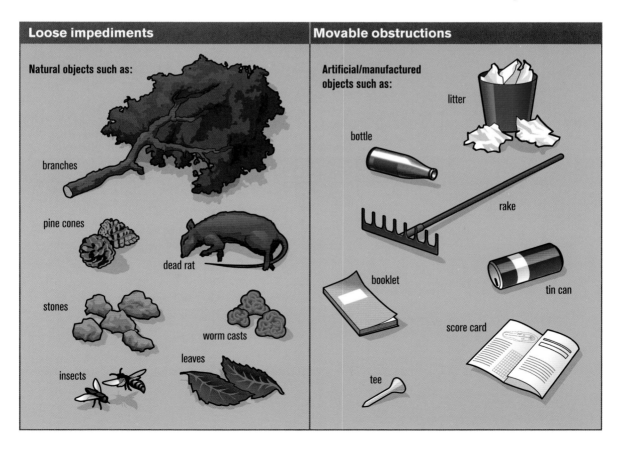

Loose impediments

Natural objects such as:

branches

pine cones

dead rat

stones

worm casts

leaves

insects

Movable obstructions

Artificial/manufactured objects such as:

litter

bottle

rake

booklet

tin can

score card

tee

Lost Ball A ball is deemed "*lost*" if:

a. It is not found or identified as his by the player within five minutes after the player's *side* or his or their *caddies* have begun to search for it; or

b. The player has made *stroke* at a *provisional ball* from the place where the original ball is likely to be or from a point nearer the *hole* than that place (see Rule 27-2b); or

c. The player has put another ball into play under penalty of stroke and distance (see Rule 27-la); or

d. The player has put another ball into play because it is known or virtually certain that the ball, which has not been found, has been moved by an *outside agency* (see Rule 18-1), is in an *obstruction* (see Rule 24-3), is in an *abnormal ground condition* (see Rule 25-1c) or is in a *water hazard* (see Rule 26-1); or

e. The player has made a *stroke* at a *substituted ball*.

Time spent in playing a *wrong ball* is not counted in the five-minute period allowed for search.

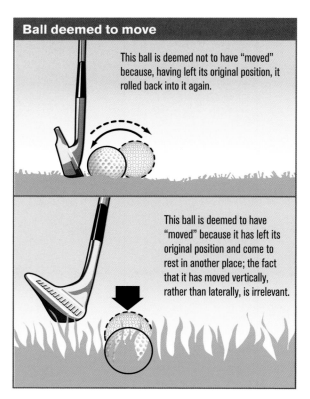

Ball deemed to move

This ball is deemed not to have "moved" because, having left its original position, it rolled back into it again.

This ball is deemed to have "moved" because it has left its original position and come to rest in another place; the fact that it has moved vertically, rather than laterally, is irrelevant.

Marker A "*marker*" is one who is appointed by the *Committee* to record a *competitor's* score in stroke play. He may be a *fellow-competitor*. He is not a *referee*.

Move or Moved A ball is deemed to have "*moved*" if it leaves its position and comes to rest in any other place.

Nearest Point of Relief The "*nearest point of relief*" is the reference point for taking relief without penalty from interference by an immovable *obstruction* (Rule 24-2), an *abnormal ground condition* (Rule 25-1) or a *wrong putting green* (Rule 25-3).

It is the point on the *course* nearest to where the ball lies:

(i) that is not nearer the *hole*, and

(ii) where, if the ball were so positioned, no interference by the condition from which relief is sought would exist for the *stroke* the player would have made from the original position if the condition were not there.

Note: In order to determine the *nearest point of relief* accurately, the player should use the club with which he would have made his next *stroke* if the condition were not there to simulate the *address* position, direction of play and swing for such a *stroke*.

Observer An "*observer*" is one who is appointed by the *Committee* to assist a *referee* to decide questions of fact and to report to him any breach of a *Rule*. An *observer* should not attend the *flagstick*, stand at or mark the position of the *hole*, or lift the ball or mark its position.

Obstructions An "*obstruction*" is anything artificial, including the artificial surfaces and sides of roads and paths and manufactured ice, except:

a. Objects defining *out of bounds*, such as walls, fences, stakes and railings;

b. Any part of an immovable artificial object that is *out of bounds*; and

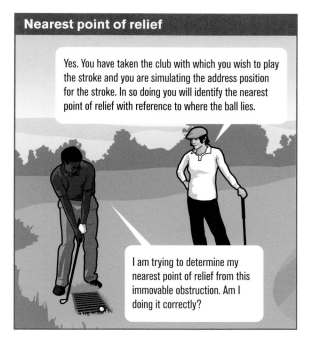

Nearest point of relief

Yes. You have taken the club with which you wish to play the stroke and you are simulating the address position for the stroke. In so doing you will identify the nearest point of relief with reference to where the ball lies.

I am trying to determine my nearest point of relief from this immovable obstruction. Am I doing it correctly?

c. Any construction declared by the *Committee* to be an integral part of the *course*.

An *obstruction* is a movable *obstruction* if it may be moved without unreasonable effort, without unduly delaying play and without causing damage. Otherwise it is an immovable *obstruction*.

> **Note:** The *Committee* may make a Local Rule declaring a movable *obstruction* to be an immovable *obstruction*.

Out of Bounds "*Out of bounds*" is beyond the boundaries of the *course* or any part of the *course* so marked by the *Committee*.

When *out of bounds* is defined by reference to stakes or a fence or as being beyond stakes or a fence, the *out of bounds* line is determined by the nearest inside points at ground level of the stakes or fence posts (excluding angled supports). When both stakes and lines are used to indicate *out of bounds*, the stakes identify *out of bounds* and the lines define *out of bounds*. When *out of bounds* is defined by a line on the ground, the line itself is *out of bounds*. The *out of bounds* line extends vertically upwards and downwards.

A ball is *out of bounds* when all of it lies *out of bounds*. A player may stand *out of bounds* to play a ball lying within bounds.

Objects defining *out of bounds* such as walls, fences, stakes and railings are not *obstructions* and are deemed to be fixed. Stakes identifying *out of bounds* are not *obstructions* and are deemed to be fixed.

> **Note 1:** Stakes or lines used to define *out of bounds* should be white.

> **Note 2:** A *Committee* may make a Local Rule declaring stakes identifying but not defining *out of bounds* to be movable *obstructions*.

Outside Agency In match play, an "*outside agency*" is any agency other than either the player's or opponent's *side*, any *caddie* of either *side*, any ball played by either *side* at the hole being played or any *equipment* of either *side*. In stroke play, an *outside agency* is any agency other than the *competitor's side*, any *caddie* of the *side*, any ball played by the *side* at the hole being played or any *equipment* of the *side*. An *outside agency* includes a *referee*, a *marker*, an *observer* and a *forecaddie*. Neither wind nor water is an *outside agency*.

Partner A "*partner*" is a player associated with another player on the same *side*.

In *threesome*, *foursome*, *best-ball* or *four-ball* play, where the context so admits, the word "player" includes his *partner* or *partners*.

Partner

A partner is a player associated with another player on the same side.

Penalty Stroke A "*penalty stroke*" is one added to the score of a player or *side* under certain *Rules*. In a *threesome* or *foursome*, *penalty strokes* do not affect the order of play.

Provisional Ball A "*provisional ball*" is a ball played under Rule 27-2 for a ball that may be *lost* outside a *water hazard* or may be *out of bounds*.

Putting Green The "*putting green*" is all ground of the hole being played that is specially prepared for putting or otherwise defined as such by the *Committee*. A ball is on the *putting green* when any part of it touches the *putting green*.

R&A The "*R&A*" means R&A Rules Limited.

Referee A "*referee*" is one who is appointed by the *Committee* to accompany players to decide questions of fact and apply the *Rules*. He must act on any breach of a *Rule* that he observes or is reported to him.

A *referee* should not attend the *flagstick*, stand at or mark the position of the *hole*, or lift the ball or mark its position.

Rub of the Green A "*rub of the green*" occurs when a ball in motion is accidentally deflected or stopped by any *outside agency* (see Rule 19-1).

Rule or Rules The term "*Rule*" includes:
a. The Rules of Golf and their interpretations as contained in Decisions on the Rules of Golf;
b. Any Conditions of Competition established by the *Committee* under Rule 33-1 and Appendix I;
c. Any Local Rules established by the *Committee* under Rule 33-8a and Appendix I; and
d. The specifications on clubs and the ball in Appendices II and III and their interpretations

contained in A Guide to the Rules on Clubs and Balls.

Side A "*side*" is a player, or two or more players who are *partners*.

Single See "*Forms of Match Play*" and "*Forms of Stroke Play*".

Stance Taking the "*stance*" consists in a player placing his feet in position for and preparatory to making a *stroke*.

Stipulated Round The "*stipulated round*" consists of playing the holes of the *course* in their correct sequence, unless otherwise authorised by the *Committee*. The number of holes in a *stipulated round* is 18 unless a smaller number is authorised by the *Committee*. As to extension of *stipulated round* in match play, see Rule 2-3.

Stroke A "*stroke*" is the forward movement of the club made with the intention of striking at and moving the ball, but if a player checks his downswing voluntarily before the clubhead reaches the ball he has not made a *stroke*.

Definition of a stroke

At this point, as the player has not started his downswing, he has not begun his stroke. Once the player begins his downswing he is considered to have made a stroke, unless he checks his downswing voluntarily.

Teeing ground

The "teeing ground" is a rectangular area two club-lengths in depth stretching back from the tee-markers. A player may, if he wishes, stand outside the teeing ground to play a ball from within it.

Substituted Ball A "*substituted ball*" is a ball put into play for the original ball that was either *in play*, *lost*, *out of bounds* or lifted.

Tee A "*tee*" is a device designed to raise the ball off the ground. It must not be longer than 4 inches (101.6 mm) and it must not be designed or manufactured in such a way that it could indicate the *line of play* or influence the movement of the ball.

Teeing Ground The "*teeing ground*" is the starting place for the hole to be played. It is a rectangular area two club-lengths in depth, the front and the sides of which are defined by the outside limits of two tee-markers. A ball is outside the *teeing ground* when all of it lies outside the *teeing ground*.

Three-Ball See "*Forms of Match Play*".

Threesome See "*Forms of Match Play*".

Through the Green "*Through the green*" is the whole area of the *course* except:

a. The *teeing ground* and *putting green* of the hole being played; and
b. All *hazards* on the *course*.

Water Hazard A "*water hazard*" is any sea, lake, pond, river, ditch, surface drainage ditch or other open water course (whether or not containing water) and anything of a similar nature on the *course*. All ground and water within the margin of a *water hazard* are part of the *water hazard*.

When the margin of a *water hazard* is defined by stakes, the stakes are inside the *water hazard*, and the margin of the *hazard* is defined by the nearest outside points of the stakes at ground level. When both stakes and lines are used to indicate a *water hazard*, the stakes identify the *hazard* and the lines define the *hazard* margin. When the margin of a *water hazard* is defined by a line on the ground, the line itself is in the *water hazard*. The margin of a *water hazard* extends vertically upwards and downwards.

A ball is in a *water hazard* when it lies in or any part of it touches the *water hazard*.

Stakes used to define the margin of or identify a *water hazard* are *obstructions*.

Note 1: Stakes or lines used to define the margin of or identify a *water hazard* must be yellow.

Note 2: The *Committee* may make a Local Rule prohibiting play from an environmentally-sensitive area defined as a *water hazard*.

Wrong Ball A "*wrong ball*" is any ball other than the player's:
- *ball in play*;
- *provisional ball*; or
- second ball played under Rule 3-3 or Rule 20-7c in stroke play;

and includes:
- another player's ball;
- an abandoned ball; and
- the player's original ball when it is no longer *in play*.

Note: *Ball in play* includes a ball *substituted* for the *ball in play*, whether or not the substitution is permitted.

Wrong Putting Green A "*wrong putting green*" is any *putting green* other than that of the hole being played. Unless otherwise prescribed by the *Committee*, this term includes a practice *putting green* or pitching green on the *course*.

Rules Incident

During his quarter-final match with Thomas Levet at the 2004 HSBC World Match Play at Wentworth, Padraig Harrington's ball lay close to a tree on the 9th hole. The Irishman was concerned that the branches of the tree might interfere with the area of his intended swing, but seemed to have convinced himself prior to addressing the ball that there would not be any interference. On taking his backswing, the player's club struck a part of the tree and, although Harrington began his downswing, he decided during the downswing not to strike the ball. Although unable to stop the

club before it reached the ball, the player adjusted his swing to intentionally swing over the ball.

Harrington advised the referee walking with the match that he had altered the path of the downswing deliberately in order to miss the ball. In accordance with the provisions of Decision 14/1.5, the referee decided that Harrington had not made a stroke as his intention to strike the ball ceased during the downswing. In addition, as nothing had been done to improve the area of the player's intended swing when he clipped the tree, there was no penalty under Rule 13-2.

However, the incident did not end there. When Harrington actually came to play the stroke, his hand struck the tree on his follow-through. With the permission of the referee (under Rule 6-8a), Harrington discontinued play for a few minutes to receive medical attention for a bleeding thumb. Decision 6-8a/3 confirms that it would be reasonable for the Committee to allow a player 10 to 15 minutes to recuperate from such a physical problem.

Not only was Padraig Harrington's downswing hampered by the trees but also his follow-through as his hand struck the tree.

SECTION 3
THE RULES OF PLAY

RULE 1

THE GAME

Definitions

All defined terms are in *italics* and are listed alphabetically in the Definitions section – see pages 13–24.

1-1 General

The Game of Golf consists of playing a ball with a club from the *teeing ground* into the *hole* by a *stroke* or successive *strokes* in accordance with the *Rules*.

1-2 Exerting Influence on Ball

A player or *caddie* must not take any action to influence the position or the movement of a ball except in accordance with the *Rules*.

(Removal of loose impediment – see Rule 23-1)

(Removal of movable obstruction – see Rule 24-1)

* Penalty

For breach of Rule 1-2:

Match play – Loss of hole; **Stroke play** – Two strokes.

* In the case of a serious breach of Rule 1-2, the *Committee* may impose a penalty of disqualification.

Match play: agreement to consider hole halved

How about a half?

Good idea, let's move on to the next hole.

An agreement to halve a hole being played is not an agreement to waive the Rules.

Note

A player is deemed to have committed a serious breach of Rule 1-2 if the *Committee* considers that his act of influencing the position or movement of the ball has allowed him or another player to gain a significant advantage or has placed another player, other than his *partner*, at a significant disadvantage.

1-3 Agreement to Waive Rules

Players must not agree to exclude the operation of any *Rule* or to waive any penalty incurred.

Penalty

For breach of Rule 1-3:
Match play – Disqualification of both *sides*; **Stroke play** – Disqualification of *competitors* concerned.
(Agreeing to play out of turn in stroke play – see Rule 10-2c)

1-4 Points Not Covered by Rules

If any point in dispute is not covered by the *Rules*, the decision should be made in accordance with equity.

RULE 1

INCIDENTS

During the 2006 Open de France, Michael Campbell was leading the tournament standing on the 17th tee of his third round. His first shot from the tee came to rest out of bounds. His second shot from the tee was deflected by a spectator standing out of bounds and came to rest in-bounds, but Campbell, unable to tell for sure whether the ball was in or out of bounds, played a provisional ball in accordance with Rule 27-2.

Campbell found the second ball he had played from the tee in-bounds, but by this time Rules officials had received reports from television personnel that the ball while still in motion may have been deliberately kicked by the spectator from an out of bounds position back into bounds. The Note to Rule 19-1 provides that, if the Committee determines that a player's ball in motion has been deliberately deflected by an outside agency, Rule 1-4 (equity) applies to the player. What this means is that the Committee has to determine where the ball would have come to rest had the outside agency not deliberately deflected it.

Without the benefit of television pictures it was impossible for the Rules official on the spot to make a decision as to whether the ball had been deliberately deflected (and, if so, whether it would have remained out of bounds in any case) or whether, without the deflection, there was a chance that the ball could have come back into bounds. In view of the fact that Campbell had played a provisional ball, the officials instructed him to play out the hole with the ball that had been deflected back into bounds and also with the provisional ball, in accordance with Rule 3-3.

At the conclusion of his round, Campbell reviewed the footage with the Chief Referee. The Chief Referee concluded that the player's ball had been deliberately deflected but that, in view of the nature of the terrain at the spot where the ball was deflected, the ball would have come back into bounds even without the interference of the spectator. Therefore, in equity, the player was entitled to play

Equity: some examples

Distractions are commonplace, but some problems less so. Wildlife needs to be protected and sometimes so does the golfer.

Ball comes to rest near bees' nest. Player is entitled to relief – Decision 1-4/10.

Bird's nest interferes with stroke. Player is entitled to relief – Decision 1-4/9.

Ball adheres to face of club after stroke. Player drops ball on spot where club was when ball stuck to it – Decision 1-4/2.

Ball comes to rest near snake. Player is entitled to relief – Decision 1-4/10.

the ball from the spot in-bounds where it was estimated that it would have come to rest. As a result, Campbell's score with the deflected ball counted, which gave him a six as opposed to the seven he would have scored if the provisional ball was the ball that counted.

RULE **2**

MATCH PLAY

Definitions   All defined terms are in *italics* and are listed alphabetically in the Definitions section – see pages 13–24.

2-1   General

A match consists of one *side* playing against another over a *stipulated round* unless otherwise decreed by the *Committee*.

In match play the game is played by holes.

Except as otherwise provided in the *Rules*, a hole is won by the *side* that *holes* its ball in the fewer *strokes*. In a handicap match, the lower net score wins the hole.

The state of the match is expressed by the terms: so many "holes up" or "all square", and so many "to play".

A *side* is "dormie" when it is as many holes up as there are holes remaining to be played.

2-2 Halved Hole

A hole is halved if each *side holes* out in the same number of *strokes*.

When a player has *holed* out and his opponent has been left with a *stroke* for the half, if the player subsequently incurs a penalty, the hole is halved.

2-3 Winner of Match

A match is won when one *side* leads by a number of holes greater than the number remaining to be played.

If there is a tie, the *Committee* may extend the *stipulated round* by as many holes as are required for a match to be won.

2-4 Concession of Match, Hole or Next Stroke

A player may concede a match at any time prior to the start or conclusion of that match.

A player may concede a hole at any time prior to the start or conclusion of that hole.

A player may concede his opponent's next *stroke* at any time provided the opponent's ball is at rest. The opponent is considered to have *holed* out with his next *stroke*, and the ball may be removed by either *side*.

A concession may not be declined or withdrawn.

(Ball overhanging hole – see Rule 16-2)

2-5 ### Doubt as to Procedure; Disputes and Claims

In match play, if a doubt or dispute arises between the players, a player may make a claim. If no duly authorised representative of the *Committee* is available within a reasonable time, the players must continue the match without delay. The *Committee* may consider a claim only if the player making the claim notifies his opponent (i) that he is making a claim, (ii) of the facts of the situation and (iii) that he wants a ruling. The claim must be made before any player in the match plays from the next *teeing ground* or, in the case of the last hole of the match, before all players in the match leave the *putting green*.

A later claim may not be considered by the *Committee*, unless it is based on facts previously unknown to the player making the claim and he had been given wrong information (Rules 6-2a and 9) by an opponent.

Once the result of the match has been officially announced, a later claim may not be considered by the *Committee*, unless it is satisfied that the opponent knew he was giving wrong information.

2-6 ### General Penalty

The penalty for a breach of a *Rule* in match play is loss of hole except when otherwise provided.

Status of late claim

I've just realised that my opponent should have lost the 4th when he grounded his club in the bunker.

I'm afraid such a claim had to be made before you or your opponent played from the 5th tee. The Committee can only consider a later claim if the facts were previously unknown to you.

Tony Jacklin and
Jack Nicklaus shake
hands on the 18th
green during the
1969 Ryder Cup.

RULE 2
INCIDENTS

Jack Nicklaus' concession of Tony Jacklin's putt on the final hole during the final
match of the 1969 Ryder Cup resulted in the event's first tie, and is hailed as one
of golf's finest acts of sportsmanship.

Going into the final day's competition at Royal Birkdale Golf Club in Southport,
England, the United States and Great Britain & Ireland were even at eight points
apiece. That morning's singles matches resulted in a two-point lead for Great
Britain and Ireland but the US responded in the afternoon to leave the matches
tied at 15 points each with only the final match of Nicklaus and Jacklin still on the
course. Eighteen of the 32 Ryder Cup matches went to the final hole that year,
and it was there that the three-day competition would be ultimately decided.

Nicklaus seemed to have the upper hand as Jacklin fell behind on the back nine
but the reigning Open champion Jacklin would not relent. Indeed, he eagled the
17th to go all square with Nicklaus.

At the par-5 18th, Jacklin missed his putt for birdie. Nicklaus holed his four-
footer for par leaving Jacklin with a short putt to tie Nicklaus. If he holed the putt
it would be a tie but a miss by Jacklin would result in an outright win by the
Americans.

Before Jacklin could putt, Nicklaus conceded the Englishman's putt thereby
ensuring a tie. "I don't think you would have missed that Tony," Nicklaus reportedly
said, "but under these circumstances I'd never give you the opportunity."

"The length of the putt has varied after thirty years," Jacklin has stated recently to reporters. "It's been as long as four feet. But my recollection is 20 inches. Of course, I could have missed it; there are no guarantees in golf, especially in the crucible of the Ryder Cup, but I believe I would have made it. But Jack saw the big picture, two months before I had become the first British player in 18 years to win The Open, so there was very much a pro-British fervour at the Ryder Cup in England that year. Jack saw that the putt on the last hole in 1969 meant a heck of a lot more to the Ryder Cup than who won or lost that particular match. It was a great moment."

RULE 3

STROKE PLAY

Definitions   All defined terms are in *italics* and are listed alphabetically in the Definitions section – see pages 13–24.

3-1   **General; Winner**

A stroke play competition consists of *competitors* completing each hole of a *stipulated round* or rounds and, for each round, returning a score card on which there is a gross score for each hole. Each *competitor* is playing against every other *competitor* in the competition.

Doubt as to procedure in stroke play

I'm not sure whether I can get free relief from this path. I'll play out the hole with two balls, this ball as it lies and then another ball having taken a drop away from the path. I would like the second ball to count.

That's fine, I'll record both scores and you must report to the Committee when we get in.

The competitor who plays the *stipulated round* or rounds in the fewest *strokes* is the winner.

In a handicap competition, the *competitor* with the lowest net score for the *stipulated round* or rounds is the winner.

3-2 Failure to Hole Out

If a *competitor* fails to hole out at any hole and does not correct his mistake before he makes a *stroke* on the next *teeing ground* or, in the case of the last hole of the round, before he leaves the *putting green*, **he is disqualified**.

3-3 Doubt as to Procedure

3-3 a Procedure

In stroke play, if a *competitor* is doubtful of his rights or the correct procedure during the play of a hole, he may, without penalty, complete the hole with two balls.

After the doubtful situation has arisen and before taking further action, the *competitor* must announce to his *marker* or *fellow-competitor* that he intends to play two balls and which ball he wishes to count if the *Rules* permit.

The *competitor* must report the facts of the situation to the *Committee* before returning his score card. If he fails to do so, **he is disqualified**.

Note If the *competitor* takes further action before dealing with the doubtful situation, Rule 3-3 is not applicable. The score with the original ball counts or, if the original ball is not one of the balls being played, the score with the first ball put into play counts, even if the *Rules* do not allow the procedure adopted for that ball. However, the *competitor* incurs no penalty for having played a second ball, and any *penalty strokes* incurred solely by playing that ball do not count in his score.

3-3 b Determination of Score for Hole

(i) If the ball that the *competitor* selected in advance to count has been played in accordance with the *Rules*, the score with that ball is the *competitor's* score for the hole. Otherwise, the score with the other ball counts if the *Rules* allow the procedure adopted for that ball.

(ii) If the *competitor* fails to announce in advance his decision to complete the hole with two balls, or which ball he wishes to count, the score with the original ball counts, provided it has been played in accordance with the *Rules*. If the original ball is not one of the balls being played, the first ball put into play counts, provided it has been played in accordance with the *Rules*. Otherwise, the score with the other ball counts if the *Rules* allow the procedure adopted for that ball.

Note 1 If a *competitor* plays a second ball under Rule 3-3, the *strokes* made after this Rule has been invoked with the ball ruled not to count and *penalty strokes* incurred solely by playing that ball are disregarded.

Note 2 A second ball played under Rule 3-3 is not a *provisional ball* under Rule 27-2.

3-4 **Refusal to Comply with a Rule**
If a *competitor* refuses to comply with a *Rule* affecting the rights of another *competitor*, **he is disqualified**.

3-5 **General Penalty**
The penalty for a breach of a *Rule* in stroke play is two strokes except when otherwise provided.

RULE 4 CLUBS

A player in doubt as to the conformity of a club should consult the *R&A*.

A manufacturer should submit to the *R&A* a sample of a club to be manufactured for a ruling as to whether the club conforms with the *Rules*. The sample becomes the property of the *R&A* for reference purposes. If a manufacturer fails to submit a sample or, having submitted a sample, fails to await a ruling before manufacturing and/or marketing the club, the manufacturer assumes the risk of a ruling that the club does not conform with the *Rules*.

The *R&A* reserves the right, at any time, to change the Rules relating to clubs and balls (see Appendices II and III) and make or change the interpretations relating to these Rules.

Definitions All defined terms are in *italics* and are listed alphabetically in the Definitions section – see pages 13–24.

4-1 **Form and Make of Clubs**
4-1 a **General**
The player's clubs must conform with this Rule and the provisions, specifications and interpretations set forth in Appendix II.

Note The *Committee* may require, in the conditions of a competition (Rule 33-1), that any driver the player carries must have a clubhead, identified by model and loft, that is named on the current List of Conforming Driver Heads issued by the *R&A*.

4-1 b **Wear and Alteration**
A club that conforms with the *Rules* when new is deemed to conform after wear through normal use. Any part of a club that has been purposely altered is regarded as new and must, in its altered state, conform with the *Rules*.

4-2 **Playing Characteristics Changed and Foreign Material**
4-2 a **Playing Characteristics Changed**
During a *stipulated round*, the playing characteristics of a club must not be purposely changed by adjustment or by any other means.

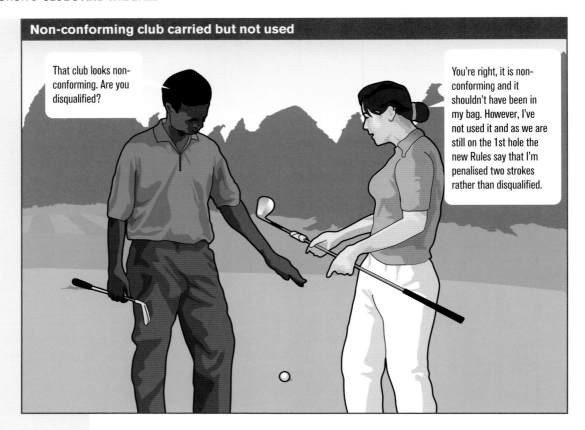

Non-conforming club carried but not used

That club looks non-conforming. Are you disqualified?

You're right, it is non-conforming and it shouldn't have been in my bag. However, I've not used it and as we are still on the 1st hole the new Rules say that I'm penalised two strokes rather than disqualified.

4-2 b   **Foreign Material**

Foreign material must not be applied to the club face for the purpose of influencing the movement of the ball.

* Penalty   **For carrying, but not making stroke with, club or clubs in breach or Rule 4-1 or 4-2:**
Match play – At the conclusion of the hole at which the breach is discovered, the state of the match is adjusted by deducting one hole for each hole at which a breach occurred; maximum deduction per round – Two holes.
Stroke play – Two strokes for each hole at which any breach occurred; maximum penalty per round – Four strokes.
Match or stroke play – In the event of a breach between the play of two holes, the penalty applies to the next hole.
Bogey and par competitions – See Note 1 to Rule 32-1a.
Stableford competitions – See Note 1 to Rule 32-1b.
* Any club or clubs carried in breach of Rule 4-1 or 4-2 must be declared out of play by the player to his opponent in match play or his *marker* or a *fellow-competitor* in stroke play immediately upon discovery that a breach has occurred. If the player fails to do so, he is disqualified.
For making stroke with club in breach of Rule 4-1 or 4-2: Disqualification.

4-3   **Damaged Clubs: Repair and Replacement**
4-3 a   **Damage in Normal Course of Play**

If, during a *stipulated round*, a player's club is damaged in the normal course of play, he may:

(i) use the club in its damaged state for the remainder of the *stipulated round*; or

(ii) without unduly delaying play, repair it or have it repaired; or

(iii) as an additional option available only if the club is unfit for play, replace the damaged club with any club. The replacement of a club must not unduly delay play and must not be made by borrowing any club selected for play by any other person playing on the *course*.

Penalty   **For breach of Rule 4-3a:** See Penalty Statement for Rule 4-4a or b, and Rule 4-4c.

Note   A club is unfit for play if it is substantially damaged, e.g. the shaft is dented, significantly bent or breaks into pieces; the clubhead becomes loose, detached or significantly deformed; or the grip becomes loose. A club is not unfit for play solely because the club's lie or loft has been altered, or the clubhead is scratched.

4-3 b   **Damage Other Than in Normal Course of Play**

If, during a *stipulated round*, a player's club is damaged other than in the normal course of play rendering it non-conforming or changing its playing characteristics, the club must not subsequently be used or replaced during the round.

4-3 c   **Damage Prior to Round**

A player may use a club damaged prior to a round provided the club, in its damaged state, conforms with the *Rules*.

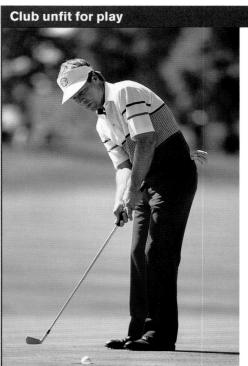

Club unfit for play

If a player's club is damaged in the normal course of play (e.g. in playing a stroke or accidentally dropping a club rendering it unfit for play), the player may, without unduly delaying play, repair it or have it repaired or replace the damaged club with any club. However, he may not borrow a club being used by anyone playing on the course.

When a club is damaged other than in the normal course of play it may not be used during the remainder of the round. Ben Crenshaw became more familiar with the provisions of Rule 4-3b at the 1987 Ryder Cup match. He was bouncing his putter along a gravel pathway in time with his step when the club's shaft broke and he spent the remainder of his match putting with various clubs.

Breach of Fourteen-club Rule in match play

I've just realised I have 15 clubs in my bag. I'll declare my 2-iron out of play, but what is the score in our match?

As we are on the 4th tee and I was already 2 up, the two-hole penalty applies to the match score, and I am now 4 up.

Damage to a club that occurred prior to a round may be repaired during the round, provided the playing characteristics are not changed and play is not unduly delayed.

| Penalty | **For breach of Rule 4-3b or c**: Disqualification. (Undue delay – see Rule 6-7) |

4-4   Maximum of Fourteen Clubs

4-4 a   Selection and Addition of Clubs

The player must not start a *stipulated round* with more than fourteen clubs. He is limited to the clubs thus selected for that round except that, if he started with fewer than fourteen clubs, he may add any number, provided his total number does not exceed fourteen.

The addition of a club or clubs must not unduly delay play (Rule 6-7) and the player must not add or borrow any club selected for play by any other person playing on the *course*.

4-4 b   Partners May Share Clubs

Partners may share clubs, provided that the total number of clubs carried by the *partners* so sharing does not exceed fourteen.

Penalty

For breach of Rule 4-4a or b, regardless of number of excess clubs carried:

Match play – At the conclusion of the hole at which the breach is discovered, the state of the match is adjusted by deducting one hole for each hole at which a breach occurred; maximum deduction per round – Two holes.

Stroke play – Two strokes for each hole at which any breach occurred; maximum penalty per round – Four strokes.

Bogey and par competitions – Note 1 to Rule 32-1a.

Stableford competitions – See Note 1 to Rule 32-1b.

4-4 c

Excess Club Declared Out of Play

Any club or clubs carried or used in breach of Rule 4-3a(iii) or Rule 4-4 must be declared out of play by the player to his opponent in match play or his *marker* or a *fellow-competitor* in stroke play immediately upon discovery that a breach has occurred. The player must not use the club or clubs for the remainder of the *stipulated round*.

Penalty

For breach of Rule 4-4c: Disqualification.

RULE 4

INCIDENTS

In the 2001 Open Championship at Royal Lytham & St Annes, Ian Woosnam played his tee-shot at the par 3 1st hole to six inches. Having started the final round as joint leader, he then tapped in for what appeared to be a birdie two – a fantastic start.

Standing on the 2nd tee, Woosnam's caddie, Miles Byrne, turned to Woosnam and said, "You're going to go ballistic. We have fifteen clubs." On the practice ground Woosnam had been testing two drivers and, rushing from the practice

Ian Woosnam is informed by the Referee in his game, John Paramor (Chief Referee, European PGA Tour), that the penalty for carrying 15 clubs is two strokes. A player is only permitted to carry a maximum of 14 clubs under Rule 4-4a.

Tiger Woods looks on in dismay as his 9-iron slips out of the grasp of his caddie and into the water at the 7th hole at the K Club. The club was returned to him on the 15th hole.

ground to the 1st tee, he had not counted his clubs to ensure that he had no more than the stipulated fourteen. So, under Rule 4-4, Ian Woosnam incurred a two-stroke penalty at the 1st hole and his birdie two became a bogey four. "I felt like I'd been kicked in the teeth," he said afterwards.

It can only be guessed how the penalty affected Woosnam's game. We do know, however, that Woosnam finished in a tie for third place on a score of 278. If he had finished on 276 he would have achieved second place on his own and be £220,000 the richer, and he would have qualified for the European team for the 34th Ryder Cup.

Another Rule 4 incident occurred at the 2006 Ryder Cup during Tiger Woods' singles match against Robert Karlsson. At the 7th hole Woods' caddie, Steve Williams, slipped on a rock while trying to dip his towel in a water hazard near the green. As a result, the 9-iron he was holding slipped out of his hand and dropped into the depths of the water.

A club that has become damaged in the normal course of play and, as a result, has become unfit for play, can be replaced during the round, provided the replacement does not delay play and the replacement club is not borrowed from any other person playing the course (Rule 4-3a). The term "damaged in the normal course of play" includes a club that has been damaged as a result of being dropped (Decision 4-3/1).

However, in Woods' case, the club had not actually been damaged at all and, therefore, Rule 4-3a was not applicable. The club was, in fact, lost and Decision 4-3/10 confirms that, if a player starts the round with fourteen clubs and then manages to lose one of his clubs, he is not entitled to replace that club.

If Woods had decided that the club was too important to leave in the water, he could have tried to retrieve it or have someone attempt to retrieve it for him, but he would have been required to continue play without delay. The five-minute search period that applies to a ball that cannot be found does not apply to a club. Woods continued play with his remaining thirteen clubs and his 9-iron was returned to him when playing the 15th hole after a diver had retrieved it.

At the Funai Classic 2005 at the Walt Disney World Resort Kevin Stadler started the final round tied for fifth place and hoping for a big pay cheque to take him from 167th on the PGA Tour's money list into the top 125, thereby avoiding a return to qualifying school. However, during play on the 1st hole, Stadler discovered that he had started the round with a wedge that had a bent shaft. He reported this to a Rules official, more with the intention of asking whether he could use it rather than anything else.

Unfortunately for Stadler, the situation was much more serious than that. Rule 4-1 (Form and Make of Clubs) states that a player's clubs must conform to the Rules and, at that time, provided a penalty of disqualification for carrying a non-conforming club. Appendix II in the Rules of Golf, which prescribes general regulations for clubs, provides that the shaft must be straight from the top of the grip to a point not more than five inches above the sole of the club. As Stadler was carrying a non-conforming club, the officials had no option but to disqualify him.

The fact that the player had not made a stroke with the club led many to criticise the severity of the Rules relating to non-conforming clubs. Even before the Stadler incident occurred, The R&A and USGA had initiated a review of Rule 4-1 in light of an almost identical situation involving Dudley Hart in 2004. As a result of this review process, the Rules were amended in 2008 to give a more lenient penalty in the situation where the player has not made a stroke with the non-conforming club (see the Penalty Statement under Rules 4-1 and 4-2). However, the penalty for making a stroke with a non-conforming club remains disqualification.

Q. Can I apply lead tape to a clubhead or shaft (a) before the start of a round; and (b) during a round?

A (a) Yes. The use of lead tape is an exception to the Rule that provides that "all adjustable parts are firmly fixed and there is no reasonable likelihood of them working loose during a round".

(b) No. A player cannot add, remove or alter lead tape during a round (Rule 4-2a). However, lead tape that becomes detached from the club in the normal course of play may be replaced (Rule 4-3a).

THE BALL

The *R&A* reserves the right, at any time, to change the Rules relating to clubs and balls (see Appendices II and III) and make or change the interpretations relating to these Rules.

Definitions All defined terms are in *italics* and are listed alphabetically in the Definitions section – see pages 13–24.

5.1 General

The ball the player plays must conform to the requirements specified in Appendix III.

Note The *Committee* may require, in the conditions of a competition (Rule 33-1), that the ball the player plays must be named on the current List of Conforming Golf Balls issued by the *R&A*.

Ball unfit for play

I think I may have cut my ball playing that bunker shot. I am going to lift it to check. Do you want to come and have a look?

Yes I do. You may change the ball if it is visibly cut, cracked or out of shape.

5-2   Foreign Material

Foreign material must not be applied to a ball for the purpose of changing its playing characteristics.

Penalty   For breach of Rule 5-1 or 5-2: Disqualification.

5-3   Ball Unfit for Play

A ball is unfit for play if it is visibly cut, cracked or out of shape. A ball is not unfit for play solely because mud or other materials adhere to it, its surface is scratched or scraped or its paint is damaged or discoloured.

If a player has reason to believe his ball has become unfit for play during play of the hole being played, he may lift the ball, without penalty, to determine whether it is unfit.

Before lifting the ball, the player must announce his intention to his opponent in match play or his *marker* or a *fellow-competitor* in stroke play and mark the position of the ball. He may then lift and examine it, provided that he gives his opponent, *marker* or *fellow-competitor* an opportunity to examine the ball and observe the lifting and replacement. The ball must not be cleaned when lifted under Rule 5-3.

If the player fails to comply with all or any part of this procedure, or if he lifts the ball without having reason to believe that it has become unfit to play during play of the hole being played, **he incurs a penalty of one stroke**.

If it is determined that the ball has become unfit for play during play of the hole being played, the player may *substitute* another ball, placing it on the spot where the original ball lay. Otherwise, the original ball must be replaced. If a player *substitutes* a ball when not permitted and makes a *stroke* at the wrongly *substituted ball*, **he incurs the general penalty for a breach of Rule 5-3**, but there is no additional penalty under this Rule or Rule 15-2.

If a ball breaks into pieces as a result of a *stroke*, the *stroke* is cancelled and the player must play a ball, without penalty, as nearly as possible at the spot from which the original ball was played (see Rule 20-5).

*Penalty	For breach of Rule 5-3: **Match play** – Loss of hole; **Stroke play** – Two strokes. *If a player incurs the general penalty for a breach of Rule 5-3, there is no additional penalty under this Rule.
Note 1	If the opponent, *marker* or *fellow-competitor* wishes to dispute a claim of unfitness, he must do so before the player plays another ball.
Note 2	If the original lie of a ball to be placed or replaced has been altered, see Rule 20–3b. (Cleaning ball lifted from putting green or under any other Rule – see Rule 21)

FAQ

Q Can I use an "x-out", "refurbished" or "practice" ball to play a round of golf?

A "X-out' is the common name used for a golf ball that a manufacturer considers to be imperfect (usually for aesthetic reasons only: for example, paint or printing errors) and, therefore, has crossed out the brand name. A "refurbished" golf ball is a second-hand ball that has been cleaned and stamped as "refurbished".

In the absence of strong evidence to suggest that an "x-out" or "refurbished" ball does not conform to the Rules, it is permissible for such a ball to be used.

The player must give his opponent, marker or fellow-competitor an opportunity to inspect a ball that a player believes is unfit for play. In some cases, a Referee may be asked to participate in this process.

However, in a competition where the Committee has adopted the condition that the ball the player uses must be named on the List of Conforming Golf Balls (see Note to Rule 5-1), such a ball may not be used, even if the ball in question (without the "x"s or without the "refurbished" stamp) does appear on the List.

In most cases, "practice" balls are simply listed conforming golf balls that have been stamped "PRACTICE" (for example, just like a ball with a golf club's logo). Such balls may be used even where the Committee has adopted the condition that the ball the player uses must be named on the List of Conforming Golf Balls.

Q Must a player announce to his opponent(s) or fellow-competitor(s) that he intends to substitute his ball between the play of two holes?
A Although such an announcement would be courteous and is good practice, a player is not required under the Rules to inform an opponent or fellow-competitor between the play of two holes that he intends to play a different ball.

Q If my ball is cut, cracked or out of shape (allowing substitution of it under Rule 5-3) do I need to substitute a ball that is similar to the original?
A No. There is no requirement under the Rules that the substituted ball must be similar to the original ball. The substituted ball must simply conform to the Rules of Golf. The situation, however, is different if the Committee has introduced the "One Ball Condition" (Appendix I, Part C, 1c), which provides that the ball the player plays must be of the same brand and model as detailed by a single entry in the current List of Conforming Golf Balls. It is recommended that such a condition be adopted only in competitions involving expert players.

RULE 6

THE PLAYER

Definitions   All defined terms are in *italics* and are listed alphabetically in the Definitions section – see pages 13–24.

6-1   Rules
The player and his *caddie* are responsible for knowing the *Rules*. During a *stipulated round*, for any breach of a *Rule* by his *caddie*, the player incurs the applicable penalty.

6-2   Handicap
6-2 a   Match Play
Before starting a match in a handicap competition, the players should determine from one another their respective handicaps. If a player begins a match having declared a handicap higher than that to which he is entitled and this affects the number of strokes given or received, **he is disqualified**; otherwise, the player must play off the declared handicap.

6-2 b   **Stroke Play**

In any round of a handicap competition, the *competitor* must ensure that his handicap is recorded on his score card before it is returned to the *Committee*. If no handicap is recorded on his score card before it is returned (Rule 6-6b), or if the recorded handicap is higher than that to which he is entitled and this affects the number of strokes received, **he is disqualified** from the handicap competition; otherwise, the score stands.

Note   It is the player's responsibility to know the holes at which handicap strokes are to be given or received.

6-3   Time of Starting and Groups

6-3 a   **Time of Starting**

The player must start at the time established by the *Committee*.

6-3 b   **Groups**

In stroke play, the *competitor* must remain throughout the round in the group arranged by the *Committee*, unless the *Committee* authorises or ratifies a change.

Penalty   For breach of **Rule 6-3:** Disqualification
(Best-ball and four-ball play – see Rules 30-3a and 31-2)

Note   The *Committee* may provide, in the conditions of a competition (Rule 33-1), that if the player arrives at his starting point, ready to play, within five minutes after his starting time, in the absence of circumstances that warrant waiving the penalty of disqualification as provided in Rule 33-7, the penalty for failure to start on time is **loss of the first hole in match play or two strokes at the first hole in stroke play** instead of disqualification.

6-4   Caddie

The player may be assisted by a *caddie*, but he is limited to only one *caddie* at any one time.

Penalty   For breach of **Rule 6-4:**
Match play – At the conclusion of the hole at which the breach is discovered, the state of the match is adjusted by deducting one hole for each hole at which a breach occurred; maximum deduction per round – Two holes.
Stroke play – Two strokes for each hole at which any breach occurred; maximum penalty per round – Four strokes.
Match or stroke play – In the event of a breach between the play of two holes, the penalty applies to the next hole.
A player having more than one *caddie* in breach of this Rule must immediately upon discovery that a breach has occurred ensure that he has no more than one *caddie* at any one time during the remainder of the *stipulated round*. Otherwise, the player is disqualified.
Bogey and par competitions – See Note 1 to Rule 32-1a.
Stableford competitions – See Note 1 to Rule 32-1b.

Note

The *Committee* may, in the conditions of a competition (Rule 33-1), prohibit the use of *caddies* or restrict a player in his choice of *caddie*.

6-5 Ball

The responsibility for playing the proper ball rests with the player. Each player should put an identification mark on his ball.

6-6 Scoring in Stroke Play

6-6 a Recording Scores

After each hole the *marker* should check the score with the *competitor* and record it. On completion of the round the *marker* must sign the score card and hand it to the *competitor*. If more than one *marker* records the scores, each must sign for the part for which he is responsible.

6-6 b Signing and Returning Score Card

After completion of the round, the *competitor* should check his score for each hole and settle any doubtful points with the *Committee*.

He must ensure that the *marker* or markers have signed the score card, sign the score card himself and return it to the *Committee* as soon as possible.

Penalty For breach of Rule 6-6b: Disqualification.

6-6 c Alteration of Score Card

No alteration may be made on a score card after the *competitor* has returned it to the *Committee*.

The responsibility for playing the proper golf ball rests with the player. Darren Clarke puts a shamrock on each of his golf balls as an identification mark.

6-6 d	**Wrong Score for Hole**

The *competitor* is responsible for the correctness of the score recorded for each hole on his score card. If he returns a score for any hole lower than actually taken, **he is disqualified**. If he returns a score for any hole higher than actually taken, the score as returned stands.

Note 1 The *Committee* is responsible for the addition of scores and application of the handicap recorded on the score card – see Rule 33-5.

Note 2 In *four-ball* stroke play, see also Rule 31-3 and 31-7a.

6-7 Undue Delay; Slow Play

The player must play without undue delay and in accordance with any pace of play guidelines that the *Committee* may establish. Between completion of a hole and playing from the next *teeing ground*, the player must not unduly delay play.

Penalty **For breach of Rule 6-7:**
Match play – Loss of hole; **Stroke play** – Two strokes.
Bogey and par competitions – See Note 2 to Rule 32-1a.
Stableford competitions – See Note 2 to Rule 32-1b.
For subsequent offence – Disqualification.

Note 1 If the player unduly delays play between holes, he is delaying the play of the next hole and, except for bogey, par and Stableford competitions (see Rule 32), the penalty applies to that hole.

Note 2 For the purpose of preventing slow play, the *Committee* may, in the conditions of a competition (Rule 33-1), establish pace of play guidelines including maximum periods of time allowed to complete a *stipulated round*, a hole or a *stroke*.
In stroke play only, the *Committee* may, in such a condition, modify the penalty for a breach of this Rule as follows:
First offence – One stroke;
Second offence – Two strokes.
For subsequent offence – Disqualification.

6-8 Discontinuance of Play; Resumption of Play

6-8 a **When Permitted**

The player must not discontinue play unless:
(i) the *Committee* has suspended play;
(ii) he believes there is danger from lightning;
(iii) he is seeking a decision from the *Committee* on a doubtful or disputed point (see Rules 2-5 and 34-3); or
(iv) there is some other good reason such as sudden illness.
Bad weather is not of itself a good reason for discontinuing play.

If the player discontinues play without specific permission from the *Committee*, he must report to the *Committee* as soon as practicable. If he does

Scoring in stroke play

COMPETITION ___SPRING STROKE PLAY___ DATE ___14 · 6 · 07___

PLAYER ___D. BROWN___   HANDICAP ___10___   Game No ___21___

Hole	Yards	Par	Stroke Index	Score	W=+ L=- H=0 POINTS	Mar Score	Hole	Yards	Par	Stroke Index	Score	W=+ L=- H=0 POINTS	Mar Score
1	312	4	17	5		6	10	369	4	12	6̶ 5	c	
2	446	4	1	4		4	11	433	4	2	3		
3	310	4	13	4		3	12	361	4	14	4		
4	370	4	9	5	b	5	13	415	4	6	5		
5	478	5	3	6			14	155	3	16	6		
8̶ 7	429	4	11	4			15	338	4	8	5		
7̶ 6	385	4	5	3			16	316	4	10	4		
8	178	3	7	4			17	191	3	4	5		
9	354	4	15	6			18	508	5	18	7		
OUT	3262			41			IN	3086	35		44		
							OUT	3262	36		41		
							TOTAL	6348	71		85		

Markers Signature ___D.B.___   e & f

Players Signature ___Bill White___

HANDICAP 10   d
NETT 75

a

Competitor's Responsibilities:

1 To record the correct handicap somewhere on the score card before it is returned to the Committee.
2 To check the gross score recorded for each hole is correct.
3 To ensure that the marker has signed the card and to countersign the card himself before it is returned to the Committee.

Committee Responsibilities:

1 Issue to each competitor a score card containing the date and the competitor's name.
2 To add the scores for each hole and apply the handicap recorded on the card.

Points to Note:

(a) Hole numbers may be altered if hole scores have been recorded in the wrong boxes.
(b) A marker need not keep a record of his own score, however it is recommended.
(c) There is nothing in the Rules that requires an alteration to be initialled.
(d) The competitor is responsible only for the correctness of the score recorded for each hole. If the competitor records a wrong total score or net score, the Committee must correct the error, without penalty to the competitor. In this instance, the Committee have added the scores for each hole and applied the handicap.
(e) There is no penalty if a marker signs the competitor's score card in the space provided for the competitor's signature, and the competitor then signs in the space provided for the marker's signature.
(f) The initialing of the score card by the competitor is sufficient for the purpose of countersignature.

so and the *Committee* considers his reason satisfactory, there is no penalty. Otherwise, **the player is disqualified**.

Exception   **In match play:** Players discontinuing match play by agreement are not subject to disqualification, unless by so doing the competition is delayed.

Note   Leaving the *course* does not of itself constitute discontinuance of play.

6-8 b   **Procedure When Play Suspended by Committee**

When play is suspended by the *Committee*, if the players in a match or group are between the play of two holes, they must not resume play until the *Committee* has ordered a resumption of play. If they have started play of a hole, they may discontinue play immediately or continue play of the hole, provided they do so without delay. If the players choose to continue play of the hole, they are permitted to discontinue play before completing it. In any case, play must be discontinued after the hole is completed.

The players must resume play when the *Committee* has ordered a resumption of play.

Penalty   For breach of Rule 6-8b: Disqualification.

Note	The *Committee* may provide, in the conditions of a competition (Rule 33-1), that in potentially dangerous situations play must be discontinued immediately following a suspension of play by the *Committee*. If a player fails to discontinue play immediately, **he is disqualified**, unless circumstances warrant waiving the penalty as provided in Rule 33-7.

6-8 c   **Lifting Ball When Play Discontinued**

When a player discontinues play of a hole under Rule 6-8a, he may lift his ball, without penalty, only if the *Committee* has suspended play or there is a good reason to lift it. Before lifting the ball the player must mark its position. If the player discontinues play and lifts his ball without specific permission from the *Committee*, he must, when reporting to the *Committee* (Rule 6-8a), report the lifting of the ball.

If the player lifts the ball without a good reason to do so, fails to mark the position of the ball before lifting it or fails to report the lifting of the ball, **he incurs a penalty of one stroke**.

6-8 d   **Procedure When Play Resumed**

Play must be resumed from where it was discontinued, even if resumption occurs on a subsequent day. The player must, either before or when play is resumed, proceed as follows:

(i) if the player has lifted the ball, he must, provided he was entitled to lift it under Rule 6-8c, place the original or a *substituted* ball on the spot from which the original ball was lifted. Otherwise, the original ball must be replaced;

Discontinuance of play

Lets take shelter for 10 minutes or so.

No, as this is stroke play we must keep going. We'll be disqualified if we take shelter just because we're getting soaked.

We are all square with two to play, but I think it is too dark to go on. Why don't we replay tomorrow?

I agree it's too dark to finish tonight. As it is match play, we can complete the round tomorrow, but we must continue from where we left off, not start another match.

Stroke play   **Match play**

(ii) if the player has not lifted his ball, he may, provided he was entitled to lift it under Rule 6-8c, lift, clean and replace the ball, or *substitute* a ball, on the spot from which the original ball was lifted. Before lifting the ball he must mark its position; or

(iii) if the player's ball or ball-marker is moved (including by wind or water) while play is discontinued, a ball or ball-marker must be placed on the spot from which the original ball or ball-marker was moved.

Note   If the spot where the ball is to be placed is impossible to determine, it must be estimated and the ball placed on the estimated spot. The provisions of Rule 20-3c do not apply.

*Penalty   **For breach of Rule 6-8d:**
Match play – Loss of hole; **Stroke play** – Two strokes.
*If a player incurs the general penalty for a breach of Rule 6-8d, there is no additional penalty under Rule 6-8c.

RULE **6**

INCIDENTS

As the ultimate testament to a player's performance on the course in a stroke-play competition, the score card must never contain a score lower than actually taken and it must be signed by the competitor, attested by the marker and returned as soon as possible to the Committee. Failure to meet any of these criteria results in disqualification.

Roberto De Vicenzo signed for a higher score than he actually made at the 1968 Masters Tournament, which did not disqualify him but it prevented the Argentinian from forcing a play-off with Bob Goalby.

Playing in front of Goalby on Sunday, De Vicenzo, the reigning Open Champion, sank a five-foot birdie putt on the 17th hole for a three. A bogey at the 18th gave him an 11-under total of 277. Goalby managed a five-footer for par at the 18th for a 66 and another 277.

However, De Vicenzo's fellow-competitor and marker, Tommy Aaron, had mistakenly given De Vicenzo a four at the 17th rather than the three. De Vicenzo had not noticed the mistake, signed and returned the score card, and rushed away from the scorer's table for press interviews. A little later, Aaron noticed the mistake and brought it to the attention of tournament officials.

Augusta National founder Bob Jones searched for a way around the ensuing ruling but none could be found. Once the score card was signed and returned, the decision under the Rules was straightforward: the higher score must stand. Goalby was the Masters Champion.

An hour later, De Vicenzo told the media, "It's my fault. Tommy feels like I feel, very bad. I think the Rule is hard." The day's drama was compounded by the fact that it was De Vincenzo's 45th birthday.

There is little doubt that one of the most unfortunate Rules incidents of recent times was the disqualification of Jesper Parnevik and Mark Roe from The 2003 Open at Royal St George's.

Jesper Parnevik and Mark Roe shake hands at the end of their third round at The 2003 Open at Royal St George's. Subsequently they learned that they had both been disqualified under Rule 6-6d, for inadvertently recording their scores on their opponent's card.

Parnevik and Roe were handed their own score cards on the 1st tee by the starter in accordance with custom and practice at The Open and consistent with the practice on the PGA European Tour. Unfortunately, the players failed to exchange score cards. This resulted in each player writing the other's score on his own card. After completing their rounds, the players checked the scores they had recorded, signed the score cards, returned them and left the recorder's area.

Rule 6-6d in the Rules of Golf provides that a player is responsible for the correctness of the score recorded for each hole on his score card. If he returns a score for a hole that is lower than actually taken, he is disqualified. At that time, Decision 6-6d/4 stipulated that, if players fail to exchange cards and this results in each player having recorded and signed for at least one score for a hole that is lower than actually taken, both players are disqualified. Therefore, the Committee had no option but to apply the Rule and disqualify Parnevik and Roe.

It was hugely disappointing that such an incident should arise during the third round of The Open, especially for Mark Roe who had played so well that day and would have been playing in one of the final groups on the Sunday.

The R&A stated at the time that the many views expressed by the golfing public on the outcome of the case would form part of The R&A's ongoing review of the Rules of Golf. In 2006, Decision 6-6d/4 was amended to provide that, in the circumstances where the players fail to exchange score cards and, as a result, return score cards that have mismatched the player's printed names with the reported scores, this should be deemed an administrative error on the part of the players and the Committee should simply correct the error by striking the names printed on the score cards and entering the name of the player whose scores are recorded on the card.

FAQ

Q Must a player enter his handicap in the box provided on the score card?

A Although under Rule 6-2b a competitor must ensure that his handicap is recorded on his score card before it is returned to the Committee, it does not stipulate where the handicap shall be recorded; as long as it appears somewhere on the card, the competitor has fulfilled his duty. Consequently, a competitor cannot be disqualified for failure to record his handicap in the "official" box provided on the score card.

Q Can a player be disqualified for not initialling any alterations made on his score card?

A A Committee cannot require that alterations made on score cards be initialled. Consequently, a player should not be disqualified for failure to do so.

Q Can a player be disqualified for an omission or error in entering his score into a computer?

A The Rules of Golf do not require a competitor to enter scores into a computer. Therefore, a competitor may not be penalised or disqualified under the Rules of Golf if the scores entered into the computer are incorrect, or indeed if he fails to enter these scores. The Committee could, however, impose a disciplinary penalty (for example, ineligibility to enter the next Club competition) under its Club regulations for failure to enter scores into a computer.

RULE 7

PRACTICE

Definitions All defined terms are in *italics* and are listed alphabetically in the Definitions section – see pages 13–24.

7-1 Before or Between Rounds

7-1 a Match Play

On any day of a match play competition, a player may practise on the competition *course* before a round.

7-1 b Stroke Play

Before a round or play-off on any day of a stroke play competition, a *competitor* must not practise on the competition *course* or test the surface of any *putting green* on the *course* by rolling a ball or roughening or scraping the surface.

When two or more rounds of a stroke play competition are to be played over consecutive days, a *competitor* must not practise between those rounds on any competition *course* remaining to be played, or test the surface of any *putting green* on such *course* by rolling a ball or roughening or scraping the surface.

Exception Practice putting or chipping on or near the first *teeing ground* before starting a round or play-off is permitted.

Penalty **For breach of Rule 7-1b:** Disqualification.

Note The *Committee* may, in the conditions of a competition (Rule 33-1), prohibit practice on the competition *course* on any day of a match play competition or permit practice on the competition *course* or part of the *course* (Rule 33-2c) on any day of or between rounds of a stroke play competition.

7-2 **During Round**

A player must not make a practice *stroke* during play of a hole.

Between the play of two holes a player must not make a practice *stroke*, except that he may practise putting or chipping on or near:

a. the *putting green* of the hole last played,

b. any practice *putting green*, or

c. the *teeing ground* of the next hole to be played in the round,

provided a practice *stroke* is not made from a *hazard* and does not unduly delay play (Rule 6-7).

Strokes made in continuing the play of a hole, the result of which has been decided, are not practice strokes.

Exception When play has been suspended by the *Committee*, a player may, prior to resumption of play, practise (a) as provided in this Rule, (b) anywhere other than on the competition *course* and (c) as otherwise permitted by the *Committee*.

Penalty **For breach of Rule 7-2:**
Match play – Loss of hole; **Stroke play** – Two strokes.
In the event of a breach between the play of two holes, the penalty applies to the next hole.

Note 1 A practice swing is not a practice *stroke* and may be taken at any place, provided the player does not breach the *Rules*.

Note 2 The *Committee* may, in the conditions of a competition (Rule 33-1), prohibit:

a. practice on or near the *putting green* of the hole last played, and

b. rolling a ball on the *putting green* of the hole last played.

Practice during a round

Practice putting and chipping on or near the tee of the next hole to be played is permitted as long as play is not delayed.

RULE **7**

INCIDENTS

After the suspension of play during the fourth round of the 2001 Players Championship at Sawgrass, both the penultimate group and the final group were required to resume play from the 10th tee. Tiger Woods, playing in the final group, was aware that the group in front would resume play first and that he would have additional time to arrive at the 10th tee.

Officials, concerned that Woods may have continued to hit practice shots on the practice range after the signal for a resumption of play had been sounded, advised Woods that such action would be in breach of Rule 7-2. Play was resumed without incident and Woods went on to win The Players Championship by one stroke from Vijay Singh.

FAQ

Q May a player practise on the competition course?

A Before a match play competition, a player may practise on the competition course unless prohibited from doing so by the Committee – see the Note to Rule 7-1. However, in stroke play, a competitor is not permitted to practise on the competition course before the competition or test the surface of any putting green unless permitted to do so by the Committee.

During a competition, a player is not permitted to play a practice stroke either during the play of a hole or between the play of two holes, except that, between the play of two holes, the player may practise putting or chipping on or near the putting green of the hole last played, and on any practice putting green or the teeing ground of the next hole to be played, provided such a practice stroke is not played from a hazard and does not unduly delay play.

RULE 8 ADVICE; INDICATING LINE OF PLAY

Definitions All defined terms are in *italics* and are listed alphabetically in the Definitions section – see pages 13–24.

8-1 Advice

During a *stipulated round*, a player must not:

a. give *advice* to anyone in the competition playing on the *course* other than his *partner*, or

b. ask for *advice* from anyone other than his *partner* or either of their *caddies*.

8-2 Indicating Line of Play

8-2 a Other Than on Putting Green

Except on the *putting green*, a player may have the *line of play* indicated to him by anyone, but no one may be positioned by the player on or close to the line or an extension of the line beyond the *hole* while the *stroke* is being made. Any mark placed by the player or with his knowledge to indicate the line must be removed before the *stroke* is made.

Exception *Flagstick* attended or held up – see Rule 17-1.

8-2 b On the Putting Green

When the player's ball is on the *putting green*, the player, his *partner* or either of their *caddies* may, before but not during the stroke, point out a line for putting, but in so doing the *putting green* must not be touched. A mark must not be placed anywhere to indicate a line for putting.

Advice

My yardage chart shows that I have 150 yards to the green from this bunker, but I'm still not sure what club to use.

Don't ask me or you'll be penalised for seeking advice.

Indicating line of play

Penalty

For breach of Rule: Match play – Loss of hole; **Stroke play** – Two strokes.

Note

The *Committee* may, in the conditions of a team competition (Rule 33-1), permit each team to appoint one person who may give *advice* (including pointing out a line for putting) to members of that team. The *Committee* may establish conditions relating to the appointment and permitted conduct of that person, who must be identified to the *Committee* before giving *advice*.

RULE 8

INCIDENTS

During the third round of the 1991 PGA Championship, while advising John Daly about the break of a putt on Crooked Stick's 11th green, Daly's caddie, Jeff "Squeeky" Medlen, accidentally touched the green with the flagstick.

As ninth alternate, Daly had been included in the Championship field when Nick Price withdrew to be present at the birth of his child and three alternates ahead of Daly declined for various reasons. The unknown Arkansan had taken the outright lead for the title after posting a 69 and 67 for the first and second rounds respectively. Playing with Bruce Lietzke on Saturday, Daly was on his way to a third round 69. At the 11th, Medlen used his hand to point out the line of Daly's first putt. In his other hand, Medlen held the flagstick and inadvertently allowed it to touch the green.

The potential breach of the Rules was televised to millions and, fortunately, videotaped for review. Alerted almost immediately to what had taken place, Rules officials met Daly at the end of the round to discuss the matter and make a decision before Daly returned his score card.

Daly, Medlen, Lietzke and Rules officials reviewed the videotape. The tape showed Medlen holding the removed flagstick and allowing it to touch the putting green about three feet to the right of the hole while indicating the line of putt with his other hand. Rule 8-2 states that, while a line for putting may be pointed out, the green shall not be touched in doing so.

After speaking with all involved and watching the tape, officials were satisfied that no penalty was incurred. Daly returned his third round card with a score of 69. The following day, he won the PGA Championship by three shots.

RULE 9 INFORMATION AS TO STROKES TAKEN

Definitions All defined terms are in *italics* and are listed alphabetically in the Definitions section – see pages 13–24.

9-1 General

The number of *strokes* a player has taken includes any *penalty strokes* incurred.

9-2 Match Play

9-2 a Information as to Strokes Taken

An opponent is entitled to ascertain from the player, during the play of a hole, the number of *strokes* he has taken and, after play of a hole, the number of *strokes* taken on the hole just completed.

9-2 b Wrong Information

A player must not give wrong information to his opponent. If a player gives wrong information, **he loses the hole**.

A player is deemed to have given wrong information if he:

(i) fails to inform his opponent as soon as practicable that he has incurred a penalty, unless **(a)** he was obviously proceeding under a *Rule* involving a penalty and this was observed by his opponent, or **(b)** he corrects the mistake before his opponent makes his next *stroke*; or

(ii) gives incorrect information during play of a hole regarding the number of *strokes* taken and does not correct the mistake before his opponent makes his next *stroke*; or

Information as to strokes taken

(iii) gives incorrect information regarding the number of *strokes* taken to complete a hole and this affects the opponent's understanding of the result of the hole, unless he corrects the mistake before any player makes a *stroke* from the next *teeing ground* or, in the case of the last hole of the match, before all players leave the *putting green*.

A player has given wrong information even if it is due to the failure to include a penalty that he did not know he had incurred. It is the player's responsibility to know the *Rules*.

9-3 Stroke Play

A *competitor* who has incurred a penalty should inform his *marker* as soon as practicable.

RULE 10 ORDER OF PLAY

Definitions All defined terms are in *italics* and are listed alphabetically in the Definitions section – see pages 13–24.

10-1 Match Play

10-1 a When Starting Play of Hole

The *side* that has the *honour* at the first *teeing ground* is determined by the order of the draw. In the absence of a draw, the *honour* should be decided by lot.

The *side* that wins a hole takes the *honour* at the next *teeing ground*. If a hole has been halved, the *side* that had the *honour* at the previous *teeing ground* retains it.

10-1 b During Play of Hole

After both players have started play of the hole, the ball farther from the *hole* is played first. If the balls are equidistant from the *hole* or their positions relative to the *hole* are not determinable, the ball to be played first should be decided by lot.

Exception Rule 30-3b (*best-ball* and *four-ball* match play).

Note When it becomes known that the original ball is not to be played as it lies and the player is required to play a ball as nearly as possible at the spot from which the original ball was last played (see Rule 20-5), the order of play is determined by the spot from which the previous *stroke* was made. When a ball may be played from a spot other than where the previous *stroke* was made, the order of play is determined by the position where the original ball came to rest.

10-1 c **Playing Out of Turn**

If a player plays when his opponent should have played, there is no penalty, but the opponent may immediately require the player to cancel the *stroke* so made and, in correct order, play a ball as nearly as possible at the spot from which the original ball was last played (see Rule 20-5).

10-2 **Stroke Play**

10-2 a **When Starting Play of Hole**

The *competitor* who has the *honour* at the first *teeing ground* is determined by the order of the draw. In the absence of a draw, the *honour* should be decided by lot.

   The *competitor* with the lowest score at a hole takes the *honour* at the next *teeing ground*. The *competitor* with the second lowest score plays next and so on. If two or more *competitors* have the same score at a hole, they play from the next *teeing ground* in the same order as at the previous *teeing ground*.

Exception Rule 32-1 (handicap bogey, par and Stableford competitions).

10-2 b **During Play of Hole**

After the *competitors* have started play of the hole, the ball farthest from the *hole* is played first. If two or more balls are equidistant from the *hole* or their positions relative to the *hole* are not determinable, the ball to be played first should be decided by lot.

Exceptions Rules 22 (ball assisting or interfering with play) and 31-4 (*four-ball* stroke play).

Note When it becomes known that the original ball is not to be played as it lies and the *competitor* is required to play a ball as nearly as possible at the spot from which the original ball was last played (see Rule 20-5), the order of play is determined by the spot from which the previous *stroke* was made. When a ball may be played from a spot other than where the previous *stroke* was made, the order of play is determined by the position where the original ball came to rest.

10-2 c **Playing Out of Turn**

If a *competitor* plays out of turn, there is no penalty and the ball is played as it lies. If, however, the *Committee* determines that *competitors* have agreed to play out of turn to give one of them an advantage, **they are disqualified**. (Making stroke while another ball in motion after stroke from putting green – see Rule 16-1f)

(Incorrect order of play in threesome and foursome stroke play – see Rule 29-3)

10-3   **Provisional Ball or Another Ball from Teeing Ground**

If a player plays a *provisional ball* or another ball from the *teeing ground*, he must do so after his opponent or *fellow-competitor* has made his first *stroke*. If more than one player elects to play a *provisional ball* or is required to play another ball from the *teeing ground*, the original order of play must be retained. If a player plays a *provisional ball* or another ball out of turn, Rule 10-1c or 10-2c applies.

RULE 10

INCIDENTS

On the second day of the 2003 Walker Cup at Ganton, the Great Britain & Ireland pairing of Gary Wolstenholme and Oliver Wilson were up against Trip Kuehne and Bill Haas of the USA in the morning foursomes.

Kuehne played first from the 2nd tee, hitting a long but wayward drive into some gorse bushes, then Wolstenholme followed with a shorter drive into a fairway bunker. When the players arrived at their balls, a search for the USA ball was ongoing. Before the end of the five-minute search period, Wilson played out of the bunker for Great Britain & Ireland and then Wolstenholme played the ball on to the green.

At this point, the USA side queried whether the home team had played out of turn as Wolstenholme may have played from closer to the hole than the point where the USA's lost ball could have been. It was ruled that, as the USA ball could not be found, its position for establishing the correct order of play had to be estimated and the match Referee decided that, on the basis of this estimation, the Great Britain & Ireland ball had been farther from the hole and therefore had not been played out of turn.

It was recognised at the time that the Rules would benefit from greater clarification in this type of situation and the Note to Rule 10-1b now provides that,

Bob Lewis, the USA 2003 Walker Cup captain, queries with the Referee walking with the match whether the Great Britain & Ireland team had played out of turn and in breach of Rule 10-1b.

when it becomes known that the original ball is not to be played as it lies (for example, if it is not found within five minutes) and the player is required to play a ball as near as possible to the spot where the original ball was last played, the order of play is determined by the spot from where the original ball was last played. Therefore, in the Walker Cup case, at the point where the USA ball became lost it would have been their turn to play as they were required to play again from the teeing ground.

RULE 11 TEEING GROUND

Definitions   All defined terms are in *italics* and are listed alphabetically in the Definitions section – see pages 13–24.

11-1   Teeing

When a player is putting a ball into play from the *teeing ground*, it must be played from within the *teeing ground* and from the surface of the ground or from a conforming *tee* in or on the surface of the ground.

For the purposes of this Rule, the surface of the ground includes an irregularity of surface (whether or not created by the player) and sand or other natural substance (whether or not placed by the player).

If a player makes a *stroke* at a ball on a non-conforming *tee*, or at a ball teed in a manor not permitted by this Rule, **he is disqualified**.

A player may stand outside the *teeing ground* to play a ball within it.

11-2   Tee-Markers

Before a player makes his first *stroke* with any ball on the *teeing ground* of the hole being played, the tee-markers are deemed to be fixed. In these circumstances, if the player moves or allows to be moved a tee-marker for the purpose of avoiding interference with his *stance*, the area of his intended swing or his *line of play*, **he incurs the penalty for a breach of Rule 13-2.**

11-3   Ball Falling off Tee

If a ball, when not in *play*, falls off a *tee* or is knocked off a *tee* by the player in *addressing* it, it may be re-teed, without penalty. However, if a *stroke* is made at the ball in these circumstances, whether the ball is moving or not, the *stroke* counts, but there is no penalty.

11-4   Playing from Outside Teeing Ground
11-4 a   Match Play

If a player, when starting a hole, plays a ball from outside the *teeing ground*, there is no penalty, but the opponent may immediately require the player to cancel the *stroke* and play a ball from within the *teeing ground*.

Playing from the wrong tee in stroke play

This doesn't look like the 7th hole. I think we are playing the wrong hole. What do we do now?

Unfortunately, we are both penalised two strokes and we must try and find the 7th tee to continue our round. Our drives on this hole do not count.

13th tee

6th green

7th tee

11-4 b   **Stroke Play**

If a *competitor,* when starting a hole, plays a ball from outside the *teeing ground,* **he incurs a penalty of two strokes** and must then play a ball from within the *teeing ground.*

If the *competitor* makes a *stroke* from the next *teeing ground* without first correcting his mistake or, in the case of the last hole of the round, leaves the *putting green* without first declaring his intention to correct his mistake, **he is disqualified.**

The *stroke* from outside the *teeing ground* and any subsequent strokes by the *competitor* on the hole prior to his correction of the mistake do not count in his score.

11-5   **Playing from Wrong Teeing Ground**

The provisions of Rule 11-4 apply.

RULE 11
INCIDENTS

At the 1990 US Open Championship, the drama and competitive tension at Medinah Country Club had been intense all week. Hale Irwin had summoned a wave of talent reflective of his 33 professional victories, which included two previous US Open victories in 1974 and 1979. Indeed, he had holed a 45-foot birdie putt on the 72nd hole of play to force an 18-hole play-off with Mike Donald whose only PGA Tour victory had come the previous year in Williamsburg, Virginia.

The players walked off the 17th green of the play-off round with Donald leading by one. On the 18th tee Mike Donald teed up in front of the markers. The walking Referee noticed, whereupon Donald was asked to re-tee the ball.

Rule 11, as it applies to stroke play, is exact. A player incurs a penalty of two strokes if he plays from outside the teeing ground, and must then play a ball from within the teeing ground. Had Donald's mistake been observed a few moments later, after he had played from ahead of the markers, the resulting two-stroke penalty would have reversed that state of the play-off and given Irwin a one-stroke lead.

The Referee's intervention prevented the breach, but Donald's bogey at the 90th hole resulted in both men scoring 74 in the play-off round. By the terms and conditions outlined in the entry form, and for the first time in its history, the US Open then moved to sudden death to determine the winner.

On the first sudden-death hole, the 91st hole of the championship, Irwin holed an eight-foot birdie putt to become the US Open's oldest winner.

Mike Donald congratulates Hale Irwin after the 19th hole of the play-off for the 1990 US Open Championship – see incident opposite.

RULE 12 — SEARCHING FOR AND IDENTIFYING BALL

Definitions All defined terms are in *italics* and are listed alphabetically in the Definitions section – see pages 13–24.

12-1 Searching for Ball; Seeing Ball

In searching for his ball anywhere on the *course*, the player may touch or bend long grass, rushes, bushes, whins, heather or the like, but only to the extent

Searching for a ball in a bunker

If a player's ball is buried in a bunker, he may search for it by probing the sand with his fingers or he may use a rake or a club. If the ball is moved, there is no penalty but it must be replaced and, if necessary, re-covered so that only part of it is visible.

necessary to find and identify it, provided that this does not improve the lie of the ball, the area of his intended *stance* or swing or his *line of play*.

A player is not necessarily entitled to see his ball when making a *stroke*.

In a *hazard*, if a ball is believed to be covered by *loose impediments* or sand, the player may remove by probing or raking with a club or otherwise, as many *loose impediments* or as much sand as will enable him to see a part of the ball. If an excess is removed, there is no penalty and the ball must be re-covered so that only a part of it is visible. If the ball is *moved* during the removal, there is no penalty; the ball must be replaced and, if necessary, re-covered. As to removal of *loose impediments* outside a *hazard*, see Rule 23-1.

If a ball lying in or on an *obstruction* or in an *abnormal ground condition* is accidentally *moved* during search, there is no penalty; the ball must be replaced, unless the player elects to proceed under Rule 24-1b, 24-2b or 25-1b as applicable. If the player replaces the ball, he may still proceed under Rule 24-1b, 24-2b or 25-1b if applicable.

If a ball is believed to be lying in water in a *water hazard*, the player may probe for it with a club or otherwise. If the ball is *moved* in probing, it must be replaced, unless the player elects to proceed under Rule 26-1. There is no penalty for causing the ball to *move,* provided the movement of the ball was directly attributable to the specific act of probing. Otherwise, **the player incurs a *penalty stroke* under Rule 18-2a**.

Penalty   For breach of Rule 12-1:
Match play – Loss of hole; **Stroke play** – Two strokes.

12-2   **Identifying Ball**

The responsibility for playing the proper ball rests with the player. Each player should put an identification mark on his ball.

If a player has reason to believe a ball at rest is his and it is necessary to lift the ball in order to identify it, he may lift the ball, without penalty, in order to do so.

Before lifting the ball, the player must announce his intention to his opponent in match play or his *marker* or a *fellow-competitor* in stroke play and mark the position of the ball. He may then lift the ball and identify it, provided that he gives his opponent, *marker* or *fellow-competitor* an opportunity to observe the lifting and replacement. The ball must not be cleaned beyond the extent necessary for identification when lifted under Rule 12-2.

If the ball is the player's ball and he fails to comply with all or any part of this procedure, or he lifts his ball in order to identify it when not necessary to do so, **he incurs a penalty of one stroke**. If the lifted ball is the player's ball, he must replace it. If he fails to do so, **he incurs the general penalty for a breach of Rule 12-2**, but there is no additional penalty under this Rule.

Note	If the original lie of a ball to be placed or replaced has been altered, see Rule 20-3b.
*Penalty	**For breach of Rule 12-2:** **Match play** – Loss of hole; **Stroke play** – Two strokes. *If a player incurs the general penalty for a breach of Rule 12-2, there is no additional penalty under this Rule.

Identifying a ball in a bunker

A player may lift a ball in order to identify it, even if the ball lies in a bunker or water hazard. The position of the ball must be marked before it is lifted and the player must tell his opponent, fellow-competitor or marker what he intends doing before he lifts the ball. The ball must not be cleaned beyond what is necessary to identify it.

RULE 12

INCIDENTS

Golf balls can be very difficult to identify. At the 2003 Dubai Desert Classic, Alastair Forsyth's ball lodged in a palm tree. It subsequently moved slightly before the Rules official had reached the scene, and then it could not be readily identified.

While playing in the 2003 Dubai Desert Classic at the Emirates Golf Club, Alastair Forsyth's ball lodged in a tree at a spot where it could not be reached. When the player initially arrived at the ball, he was able to see that the ball was the make and number that he was playing with and he called for a ruling in order to clarify his relief options.

When the Rules official arrived at the scene, Forsyth pointed out the ball in the tree. However, by this time the ball had moved its position slightly and the markings were no longer visible. The official questioned whether Forsyth actually knew that the ball was his, but the Scotsman, with the support of his fellow-competitors, was able to advise the official that when he had first reached the ball it had been identifiable.

Satisfied with this, the official went on to explain to Forsyth that, if he deemed the ball unplayable, one of his options would be to drop a ball, under penalty of one stroke, within two club-lengths of the point on the ground immediately below the place where the ball lay in the tree, as provided in Decision 28/11. The player decided to exercise this option.

FAQ

Q Is it permissible to put an identification mark on a ball, in the form of a line that completely encircles the ball?

A Yes. Such a marking is not considered to unduly assist the player in his alignment, as a similar practice may be adopted with the manufacturer's logo.

RULE **13**

BALL PLAYED AS IT LIES

Definitions   All defined terms are in *italics* and are listed alphabetically in the Definitions section – see pages 13–24.

13-1   **General**
The ball must be played as it lies, except as otherwise provided in the *Rules*. (Ball at rest moved – see Rule 18)

13-2   **Improving Lie, Area of Intended Stance or Swing, or Line of Play**
A player must not improve or allow to be improved:
- the position or lie of his ball,
- the area of his intended *stance* or swing,
- his *line of play* or a reasonable extension of that line beyond the *hole*, or
- the area in which he is to drop or place a ball,
by any of the following actions:
- pressing a club on the ground,
- moving, bending or breaking anything growing or fixed (including immovable *obstructions* and objects defining *out of bounds*),
- creating or eliminating irregularities of surface,
- removing or pressing down sand, loose soil, replaced divots or other cut turf placed in position, or
- removing dew, frost or water.
However, the player incurs no penalty if the action occurs:
- in grounding the club lightly when *addressing the ball*,
- in fairly taking his *stance*,
- in making a *stroke* or the backward movement of his club for a *stroke* and the *stroke* is made,

Improving area of intended swing or line of play

A player must not break an interfering branch or remove sand that is off the putting green but on the line of play.

- in creating or eliminating irregularities of surface within the *teeing ground* (Rule 11-1) or in removing dew, frost or water from the *teeing ground*, or
- on the *putting green* in removing sand and loose soil or in repairing damage (Rule 16-1).

Exception   Ball in hazard – see Rule 13-4.

13-3   Building Stance

A player is entitled to place his feet firmly in taking his *stance*, but he must not build a *stance*.

13-4   Ball in Hazard; Prohibited Actions

Except as provided in the *Rules*, before making a *stroke* at a ball that is in a *hazard* (whether a *bunker* or a *water hazard*) or that, having been lifted from a *hazard*, may be dropped or placed in the *hazard*, the player must not:

a. Test the condition of the *hazard* or any similar *hazard*;

b. Touch the ground in the *hazard* or water in the *water hazard* with his hand or a club; or

c. Touch or move a *loose impediment* lying in or touching the *hazard*.

Exceptions

1 Provided nothing is done that constitutes testing the condition of the *hazard* or improves the lie of the ball, there is no penalty if the player (a) touches the ground or *loose impediments* in any *hazard* or water in a *water hazard* as a result of or to prevent falling, in removing an *obstruction*, in measuring or in marking the position of, retrieving, lifting, placing or replacing a ball under any *Rule* or (b) places his clubs in a *hazard*.

2 After making the *stroke*, if the ball is still in the *hazard* or has been lifted from the *hazard* and may be dropped or placed in the *hazard*, the player may smooth sand or soil in the *hazard*, provided nothing is done to breach Rule 13-2 with respect to his next *stroke*. If the ball is outside the *hazard* after the *stroke*, the player may smooth sand or soil in the *hazard* without restriction.

3 If the player makes a *stroke* from a *hazard* and the ball comes to rest in another *hazard*, Rule 13-4a does not apply to any subsequent actions taken in the *hazard* from which the *stroke* was made.

Note

At any time, including at *address* or in the backward movement for the *stroke*, the player may touch, with a club or otherwise, any *obstruction*, any construction declared by the *Committee* to be an integral part of the *course* or any grass, bush, tree or other growing thing.

Penalty

For breach of Rule:
Match play – Loss of hole; **Stroke play** – Two strokes.
(Searching for ball – see Rule 12-1)
(Relief for ball in water hazard – see Rule 26)

Ball in a bunker

Before making a stroke at a ball that is in a bunker the player shall not:

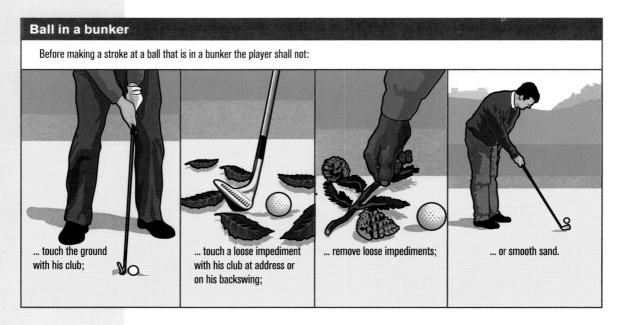

... touch the ground with his club;

... touch a loose impediment with his club at address or on his backswing;

... remove loose impediments;

... or smooth sand.

Craig Stadler returns to Torry Pines in 1995 and recreates the stroke for the assembled media.

RULE 13

INCIDENTS

In the third round of a US Tour event at Torry Pines near San Diego in 1987, when playing from underneath the branches of a tree, Craig Stadler unwittingly breached Rule 13-3 when he knelt on a towel to keep his trousers dry. Rule 13-3 states that a player is entitled to place his feet firmly in taking a stance but he must not build a stance. Prior to the incident, Decision 13-3/2 had been published stating that the act of kneeling on a towel in such circumstances was deemed to be building a stance.

A television viewer watching the incident recorded coverage of the earlier rounds and brought the incident to the attention of Tournament officials during the final round of the competition. Unfortunately, because Stadler had returned his score card for the third round containing a score for a hole lower than actually taken, he was disqualified under Rule 6-6d.

However, in 1995 Stadler had the satisfaction of returning to Torry Pines to assist in cutting down the tree that was now dying of a fungus infection. He also recreated his stroke for the assembled media.

During the final of the 2004 HSBC World Match Play Championship on the West Course at Wentworth, Lee Westwood caused some confusion among the television commentators and on-course reporters when his ball came to rest on a wooden bridge within the margins of the water hazard crossing the 7th hole.

John Paramor, the Referee for Westwood's match against Ernie Els, had been advised by his forward observer that Westwood's ball was on a bridge and, as they were walking to the ball, they discussed what the player could and could not do. Westwood reminded Paramor that they had been involved in exactly the same situation a few years earlier on the same course, only that time at the 18th hole.

With the Referee standing a reasonable distance away, the commentators were taken by surprise when Westwood took a practice swing and hit the bridge in the process with his club. They were also taken aback when he grounded his club on the bridge at address prior to making his stroke. What they did not appear to realise is that the Note to Rule 13-4 (Ball in Hazard) allows a player, at any time, including at address, to touch an obstruction with a club, even when his ball is in a hazard. A wooden bridge is an obstruction and, consequently, Westwood's action was entirely permissible. This specific point is also covered by Decision 13-4/30 in *Decisions on the Rules of Golf.*

The Note to Rule 13-4 also permits a player, whose ball lies in a hazard, to touch any construction declared by the Committee to be an integral part of the course and any grass, bush, tree or other growing thing.

However, despite the authority to touch the bridge, the other restrictions that apply under Rule 13-4 when a ball is in a hazard are still relevant when a ball lies on a bridge. Paramor was careful to ensure that Lee Westwood knew that he could not remove loose impediments from the bridge, as the loose impediments are still considered to be in the water hazard.

Match officials were crucial in the 2006 US Amateur Championship at Hazeltine National, too. Having already experienced Rules difficulties in his quarter-final match (see Rule 16 Incidents), Richie Ramsay was again involved with officials during his semi-final encounter with Webb Simpson, when, at the 16th hole, the Scotsman's ball came to rest on the dry bank of a water hazard, within the hazard margins, and was in a playable position. However, Ramsay didn't even get the chance to make a stroke at the ball, because, while preparing to play, two officials who were walking with the match, as well as a television commentator and an official who was assisting in the broadcast booth, witnessed Ramsay ground his club in breach of Rule 13-4b. All confirmed that Ramsay, while busy concentrating on how best to execute the stroke, had, unknown to himself, grounded his club while addressing his ball in the hazard.

Lee Westwood hits his ball that had been lying on a bridge in a water hazard at Wentworth.

Michelle Wie infringed Rule 13-4c when she touched some loose moss in a bunker when taking her backswing at the 2006 Women's British Open.

One up after the loss-of-hole penalty had been applied, Ramsay remained stoical for the last two holes, winning one up to progress to the final.

Michelle Wie, too, was left to count the cost of a careless error during the second round of the 2006 Women's British Open. Her ball came to rest in a greenside bunker at the 14th hole, but there was a piece of loose moss in the sand just behind her ball. Rule 13-4c provides that a player cannot touch or move a loose impediment lying in a hazard prior to the stroke, and Wie was careful not to touch the moss while she was addressing the ball. However, when taking her backswing, Wie touched the moss. As the "stroke" begins only once the player has begun the forward movement of the club (see Definition of "stroke"), the player was in breach of Rule 13-4c and, as a result, incurred a two-stroke penalty.

Despite taking two shots to extricate himself from a greenside bunker on the 10th at Sawgrass, Stephen Ames went on to win the 2006 Players' Championship by six shots.

During play of the 10th hole in the fourth round of the 2006 Players' Championship, eventual winner Stephen Ames' second shot came to rest in a greenside bunker. He failed to extricate the ball with his first attempt, and, while his ball was still in the bunker, he smoothed footprints with his feet in the area from where he played his first stroke in the bunker.

Generally, a player is not entitled to test the condition of a hazard or touch the ground in the hazard with his club while his ball is lying in the hazard (Rule 13-4). However, Exception 2 to Rule 13-4 states that, "After making the stroke, if the ball is still in the hazard or has been lifted from the hazard and may be dropped or placed in the hazard, the player may smooth sand or soil in the hazard, provided nothing is done to break Rule 13-2 with respect to the next stroke."

The area that was smoothed by Ames was not close enough to the ball's new position to improve the lie of the ball or the area of his intended stance or swing in breach of Rule 13-2. Consequently, Ames was not penalised for his actions.

It is important to note that Exception 2 applies only to the act of smoothing as it is considered that players should be encouraged to tidy up the bunker. However, if a player, between strokes in a bunker, hits the sand with his club in anger there is a penalty of loss of hole or two strokes under Rule 13-4 (see Decision 13-4/35).

RULE 14 STRIKING THE BALL

Definitions All defined terms are in *italics* and are listed alphabetically in the Definitions section – see pages 13–24.

14-1 Ball to be Fairly Struck At
The ball must be fairly struck at with the head of the club and must not be pushed, scraped or spooned.

14-2 Assistance
In making a *stroke*, a player must not:
a. Accept physical assistance or protection from the elements; or
b. Allow his *caddie*, his *partner* or his *partner's caddie* to position himself on or close to an extension of the *line of play* or the *line of putt* behind the ball.

Penalty   **For breach of Rule 14-1 or 14-2:**
Match play – Loss of hole; **Stroke play** – Two strokes.

14-3 Artificial Devices, Unusual Equipment and Unusual Use of Equipment
The *R&A* reserves the right, at any time, to change the Rules relating to artificial devices, unusual *equipment* and the unusual use of *equipment* and to make or change the interpretations relating to these Rules.

Ball to be fairly struck at with clubhead

A player may strike the ball with the back or toe of the clubhead.

A player in doubt as to whether use of an item would constitute a breach of Rule 14-3 should consult the *R&A*.

A manufacturer should submit to the *R&A* a sample of an item to be manufactured for a ruling as to whether its use during a *stipulated round* would cause a player to be in breach of Rule 14-3. The sample becomes the property of the *R&A* for reference purposes. If a manufacturer fails to submit a sample or, having submitted a sample, fails to await a ruling before manufacturing and/or marketing the item, the manufacturer assumes the risk of a ruling that use of the item would be contrary to the *Rules*.

Paul Broadhurst's caddie holds onto Broadhurst's trousers during a practice round for the 2006 Open Championship, to prevent the player falling into the bunker. Broadhurst would have incurred a two-stroke penalty if this had happened in the actual Championship for allowing someone to give him physical assistance while making a stroke.

Except as provided in the *Rules*, during a *stipulated round* the player must not use any artificial device or unusual *equipment*, or use any *equipment* in an unusual manner:

a. That might assist him in making a *stroke* or in his play; or

b. For the purpose of gauging or measuring distance or conditions that might affect his play; or

c. That might assist him in gripping the club, except that:

(i) plain gloves may be worn;

(ii) resin, powder and drying or moisturising agents may be used; and

(iii) a towel or handkerchief may be wrapped around the grip.

Exceptions

1 A player is not in breach of this Rule if (**a**) the *equipment* or device is designed for or has the effect of alleviating a medical condition, (**b**) the player has a legitimate medical reason to use the *equipment* or device, and (**c**) the *Committee* is satisfied that its use does not give the player any undue advantage over other players.

2 A player is not in breach of this Rule if he uses *equipment* in a traditionally accepted manner.

Penalty

For breach of Rule 14-3: Disqualification.

Note

The *Committee* may make a Local Rule allowing players to use devices that measure or gauge distance only.

14-4   **Striking the Ball More Than Once**

If a player's club strikes the ball more than once in the course of a *stroke*, the player must count the *stroke* and **add *a penalty stroke,*** making two *strokes* in all.

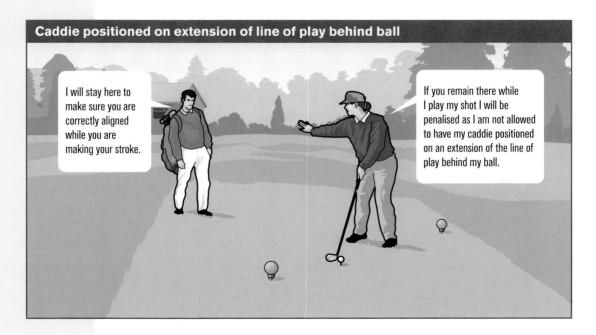

Caddie positioned on extension of line of play behind ball

14-5 Playing Moving Ball

A player must not make a *stroke* at his ball while it is moving.

Exceptions

- Ball falling off *tee* – Rule 11-3
- Striking the ball more than once – Rule 14-4
- Ball moving in water – Rule 14-6

When the ball begins to *move* only after the player has begun the *stroke* or the backward movement of his club for the *stroke*, he incurs no penalty under this Rule for playing a moving ball, but he is not exempt from any penalty under the following Rules:

- Ball at rest *moved* by player – Rule 18-2a
- Ball at rest moving after *address* – Rule 18-2b

(Ball purposely deflected or stopped by player, partner or caddie – see Rule 1-2)

14-6 Ball Moving in Water

When a ball is moving in water in a *water hazard*, the player may, without penalty, make a *stroke*, but he must not delay making his *stroke* in order to allow the wind or current to improve the position of the ball. A ball moving in water in a *water hazard* may be lifted if the player elects to invoke Rule 26.

Penalty

For breach of Rule 14-5 or 14-6:
Match play – Loss of hole; **Stroke play** – Two strokes.

RULE 14
INCIDENTS

On a rainy day at the 1995 British Masters at Collingtree Park, Domingo Hospital's first putt on the 11th hole came to rest just a few inches from the hole. His caddie walked with him holding an umbrella over Hospital. Unfortunately, as Hospital putted out his caddie still had the umbrella over his head and, therefore, the player incurred a penalty of two strokes under Rule 14-2a for accepting protection from the elements.

If Hospital had held the umbrella himself he would not have incurred any penalty as a player may protect himself from the elements. However, he must not accept such protection from anyone else.

Jeong Jang's misdemeanour occurred during the third round of the 2006 US Women's Open, when she attempted to hit the ball out of thick rough just off the 18th fairway. Immediately on making the stroke, television commentators remarked that it looked as though the player had hit the ball twice during the course of the stroke. According to Rule 14-4, a player cannot hit a ball more than once during a stroke, and if it happens the player counts one stroke but must add a one-stroke penalty.

In Jang's case the evidence that she had indeed hit the ball twice was not conclusive, so her swing sequence was reviewed several times on television replays. The initial ruling by the walking officials was that they did not feel Jang had struck her ball twice on the same swing. Nor did Jang and her caddie believe she had struck the ball twice, even though her caddie had asked her immediately after her swing whether she had done so. However, some doubt remained and, on a sophisticated plasma screen provided by NBC, further replays were cued up for review by USGA officials. The video was run again and again before it was determined conclusively that the Korean had definitely hit her ball twice. Jang was alerted that she would have a penalty of one stroke. Thus, she was given a seven on the 18th hole of her third round.

At no point did USGA Rules officials believe Jang had tried to mislead anyone. It was obvious that she believed that she had hit the ball once, although repeated replays proved that the one-stroke penalty was deserved.

Q Am I permitted to use the following during a stipulated round?
(a) a distance-measuring device, for example, a range-finder or GPS;
(b) a compass; and
(c) a pair of binoculars?
A (a) No. Rule 14-3 provides that "during a stipulated round the player shall not use any artificial device or unusual equipment ... for the purpose of gauging or measuring distance or conditions which might affect his play". However, the Committee may, in the Local Rules, permit such distance-measuring devices – see Appendix I, Part B for the Specimen Local Rule.
(b) No. Using a compass would be contrary to Rule 14-3.
(c) Yes. Binoculars that have no range-finder attachments or markings are not artificial devices in terms of Rule 14-3.

Q Can I use a pair of washing-up gloves during the course of a round?
A Rule 14-3 states that "plain gloves" may be worn to assist gripping the club – the type of glove is irrelevant. The R&A's equipment guidelines provide that a "plain glove" is one whereby the palm and gripping surface of the fingers consists of smooth material, as determined by a finger test. Therefore, provided the gripping surface of the washing-up gloves are smooth, such gloves can be worn.

RULE 15 SUBSTITUTED BALL; WRONG BALL

Definitions All defined terms are in *italics* and are listed alphabetically in the Definitions section – see pages 13–24.

15-1 General
A player must hole out with the ball played from the *teeing ground*, unless the ball is *lost* or *out of bounds* or the player *substitutes* another ball, whether or not substitution is permitted (see Rule 15-2). If a player plays a *wrong ball*, see Rule 15-3.

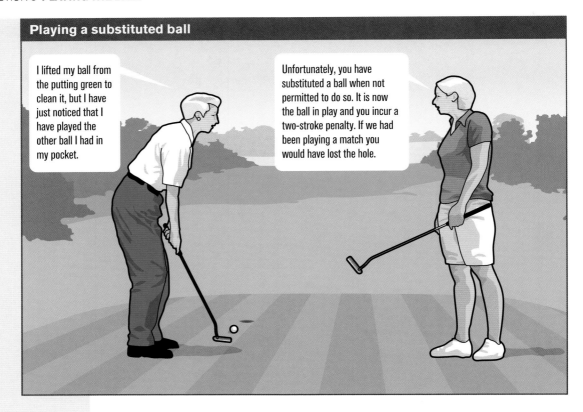

Playing a substituted ball

I lifted my ball from the putting green to clean it, but I have just noticed that I have played the other ball I had in my pocket.

Unfortunately, you have substituted a ball when not permitted to do so. It is now the ball in play and you incur a two-stroke penalty. If we had been playing a match you would have lost the hole.

15-2 Substituted Ball

A player may *substitute* a ball when proceeding under a *Rule* that permits the player to play, drop or place another ball in completing the play of a hole. The *substituted ball* becomes the *ball in play*.

If a player *substitutes* a ball when not permitted to do so under the *Rules*, that *substituted ball* is not a *wrong ball*; it becomes the *ball in play*. If the mistake is not corrected as provided in Rule 20-6 and the player makes a *stroke* at a wrongly *substituted ball*, **he loses the hole in match play or incurs a penalty of two strokes in stroke play under the applicable Rule** and, in stroke play, must play out the hole with the *substituted ball*.

Exception If a player incurs a penalty for making a *stroke* from a wrong place, there is no additional penalty for substituting a ball when not permitted.
(Playing from wrong place – see Rule 20-7)

15-3 Wrong Ball

15-3 a Match Play

If a player makes a *stroke* at a *wrong ball*, **he loses the hole**.

If the *wrong ball* belongs to another player, its owner must place a ball on the spot from which the *wrong ball* was first played.

If the player and opponent exchange balls during the play of a hole, the first to make a *stroke* at a *wrong ball* loses the hole; when this cannot be determined, the hole must be played out with the balls exchanged.

Playing a wrong ball in stroke play

Exception There is no penalty if a player makes a *stroke* at a *wrong ball* that is moving in water in a *water hazard*. Any *strokes* made at a *wrong ball* moving in water in a *water hazard* do not count in the player's score. The player must correct his mistake by playing the correct ball or by proceeding under the *Rules*.

15-3 b **Stroke Play**

If a *competitor* makes a *stroke* or *strokes* at a *wrong ball*, **he incurs a penalty of two strokes**.

The *competitor* must correct his mistake by playing the correct ball or by proceeding under the *Rules*. If he fails to correct his mistake before making a *stroke* on the next *teeing ground* or, in the case of the last hole of the round, fails to declare his intention to correct his mistake before leaving the *putting green*, **he is disqualified**.

Strokes made by a *competitor* with a *wrong ball* do not count in his score. If the *wrong ball* belongs to another *competitor*, its owner must place a ball on the spot from which the *wrong ball* was first played.

Exception There is no penalty if a *competitor* makes a *stroke* at a *wrong ball* that is moving in water in a *water hazard*. Any *strokes* made at a *wrong ball* moving in water in a *water hazard* do not count in the *competitor's* score.

(Lie of ball to be placed or replaced altered – see Rule 20-3b)

(Spot not determinable – see Rule 20-3c)

RULE 15

INCIDENTS

At the 2001 Compass Group English Open at Forest of Arden, playing the 17th hole in the last round, Raymond Russell marked the position of his ball on the putting green and threw it to his caddie to clean as usual. Unfortunately, his caddie failed to catch the ball and the ball went into the lake at the side of the green. On being informed that if he substituted a ball in order to finish the hole he would be penalised two strokes under Rule 15-2, his caddie took off his shoes and socks and lowered himself into the lake to try to find the ball in the murky water. After a short while, and with players on the fairway waiting to play their approach shots to the green, it was clear that the ball would not be found and, so, Russell had to substitute a ball and incurred a two-stroke penalty.

At the 4th hole of the last round of The Players' Championship in 2004 at Sawgrass, Ian Poulter picked up his ball on the putting green, after marking its position, but he lost his grip on it and the ball went into the nearby lake. He would have incurred a two-stroke penalty as experienced by Raymond Russell, however, Kam Bhambra, his fitness coach, was watching and stripped down to his boxer shorts, jumped into the water, and retrieved Poulter's ball. "It was the first ball I found," he said. "I was a bit worried about alligators, but duty called." Poulter parred the hole after avoiding the two-stroke penalty. This saved him from dropping twenty places on the leaderboard, which would have resulted in a loss of $20,000 in prize money.

When Raymond Russell's caddie failed to find his ball, which had accidentally rolled into the lake at Forest of Arden, Russell received a two-stroke penalty as he had to substitute another ball to enable him to complete the hole.

RULE 16 THE PUTTING GREEN

Definitions All defined terms are in *italics* and are listed alphabetically in the Definitions section – see pages 13–24.

16-1 General

16-1 a Touching Line of Putt

The *line of putt* must not be touched except:

(i) the player may remove *loose impediments*, provided he does not press anything down;

(ii) the player may place the club in front of the ball when *addressing* it, provided he does not press anything down;

(iii) in measuring – Rule 18-6;

(iv) in lifting or replacing the ball – Rule 16-1b;

(v) in pressing down a ball-marker;

(vi) in repairing old *hole* plugs or ball marks on the *putting green* – Rule 16-1c; and

(vii) in removing movable *obstructions* – Rule 24-1.

(Indicating line for putting on putting green – see Rule 8-2b)

16-1 b Lifting and Cleaning Ball

A ball on the *putting green* may be lifted and, if desired, cleaned. The position of the ball must be marked before it is lifted and the ball must be replaced (see Rule 20-1).

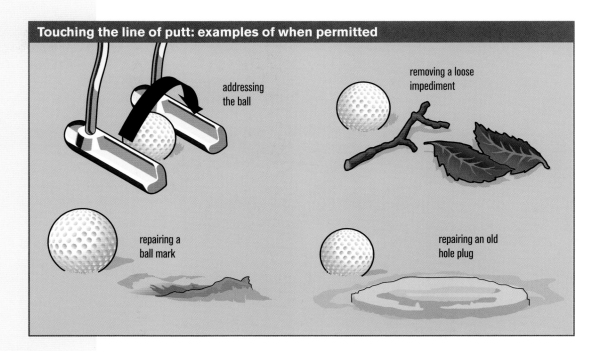

Touching the line of putt: examples of when permitted

addressing the ball

removing a loose impediment

repairing a ball mark

repairing an old hole plug

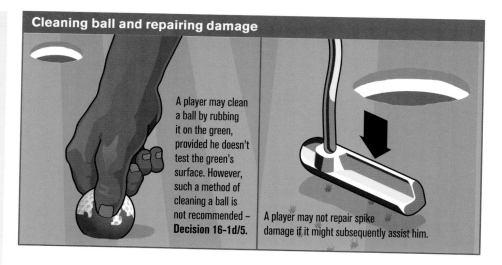

Cleaning ball and repairing damage

A player may clean a ball by rubbing it on the green, provided he doesn't test the green's surface. However, such a method of cleaning a ball is not recommended – **Decision 16-1d/5.**

A player may not repair spike damage if it might subsequently assist him.

16-1 c **Repair of Hole Plugs, Ball Marks and Other Damage**

The player may repair an old *hole* plug or damage to the *putting green* caused by the impact of a ball, whether or not the player's ball lies on the *putting green*. If a ball or ball-marker is accidentally *moved* in the process of the repair, the ball or ball-marker must be replaced. There is no penalty, provided the movement of the ball or ball-marker is directly attributable to the specific act of repairing an old *hole* plug or damage to the *putting green* caused by the impact of a ball. Otherwise, Rule 18 applies.

Any other damage to the *putting green* must not be repaired if it might assist the player in his subsequent play of the hole.

16-1 d **Testing Surface**

During the *stipulated round*, a player must not test the surface of any *putting green* by rolling a ball or roughening or scraping the surface.

Exception

Between the play of two holes, a player may test the surface of any practice *putting green* and the *putting green* of the hole last played, unless the *Committee* has prohibited such action (see Note 2 to Rule 7-2).

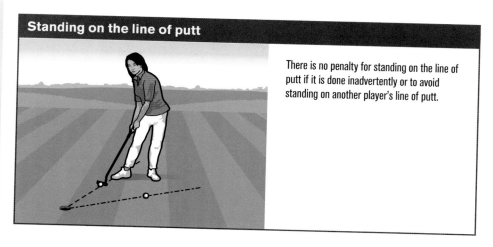

Standing on the line of putt

There is no penalty for standing on the line of putt if it is done inadvertently or to avoid standing on another player's line of putt.

Removing loose impediments from the line of putt

Can I remove these leaves using my cap rather than my hand?

Yes, loose impediments can be removed from your line of putt by any means provided you do not press anything down.

16-1 e **Standing Astride or on Line of Putt**
The player must not make a *stroke* on the *putting green* from a *stance* astride, or with either foot touching, the *line of putt* or an extension of that line behind the ball.

Exception There is no penalty if the *stance* is inadvertently taken on or astride the *line of putt* (or an extension of that line behind the ball) or is taken to avoid standing on another player's *line of putt* or prospective *line of putt.*

16-1 f **Making Stroke While Another Ball in Motion**
The player must not make a *stroke* while another ball is in motion after a *stroke* from the *putting green*, except that if a player does so, there is no penalty if it was his turn to play.
(Lifting ball assisting or interfering with play while another ball in motion – see Rule 22)

Penalty **For breach of Rule 16-1:**
Match play – Loss of hole; **Stroke play** – Two strokes.
(Position of caddie or partner – see Rule 14-2)
(Wrong putting green – see Rule 25-3)

16-2 **Ball Overhanging Hole**
When any part of the ball overhangs the lip of the *hole*, the player is allowed enough time to reach the *hole* without unreasonable delay and an additional ten seconds to determine whether the ball is at rest. If by then the ball has not fallen into the *hole*, it is deemed to be at rest. If the ball subsequently falls into the *hole*, the player is deemed to have *holed* out with his last *stroke*, and **must**

add a *penalty stroke* to his score for the hole; otherwise, there is no penalty under this Rule.

(Undue delay – see Rule 6-7)

RULE 16 INCIDENTS

The Rule dealing with a ball overhanging the hole was revised as a result of an incident involving Denis Watson during play of the 8th hole in the first round of the 1985 US Open at Oakland Hills Country Club.

From 10 feet, Watson putted and his ball stopped on the lip of the hole. After waiting an extended period of time, the ball fell in. Subsequently, Watson was told to add two penalty strokes to his score for undue delay as described at the time in Rule 16-1h.

The severe ramification of the penalty would not be clear for three more days when Watson would finish just one stroke behind the champion, Andy North.

In 1988, the Rule was moved to Rule 16-2 and a one-stroke penalty assigned to any breach.

At the 2004 Shell Houston Open, Thomas Levet's ball came to rest overhanging the edge of the hole after the player had putted it from just off the green at a par-3. Having walked promptly to the hole, the Frenchman began to count down the seconds on the fingers of his hands. Levet knew that Rule 16-2 allowed him to wait ten seconds to see if the ball would drop into the hole. Should the ball drop into the hole within the ten-second period, then he would have scored a birdie two. However, should the ball fall into the hole after the ten-second period had elapsed, Levet would have to add a penalty stroke to his score, giving him a three.

Just a moment after Levet had counted off the fingers on both hands, his ball toppled into the hole. It then became a question of whether his personal ten-second countdown had been accurate and whether television pictures might be able to establish if, in fact, Levet had counted too quickly. Luckily for Levet, Rules officials were able to review footage of the incident, which demonstrated clearly that his own count had been too quick and that the ball had fallen into the hole well within the ten-second period provided for in Rule 16-2. The fortunate Frenchman had therefore scored a two.

However, had the television evidence not been available and had there not been a more accurate timing taken by any witnesses to the incident, Levet's own count would have had to be taken as accurate, resulting in a one-stroke penalty.

In 2006, on the way to becoming the first Scotsman since 1898 to win the US Amateur Championship, Richie Ramsay had more than his fair share of Rules difficulties. The first issue arose at the 17th hole during his quarter-final match with Californian Rickie Fowler, when Ramsay's caddie, a 17-year-old high-school student Thomas Buller, attempted to point out where he thought Ramsay should hit his 20-foot birdie putt. In so doing, Buller touched his player's line of putt, in breach of Rule 16-1.

Rule 6-1 provides that, for any breach of a Rule by his caddie, the player incurs the applicable penalty and, consequently, a loss-of-hole penalty was applied to Ramsay. The young caddie must have been very relieved when the Scotsman managed to win the match at the third extra hole.

FAQ

Q What are the Rules concerning the location of the hole on the putting green?
A The location of the hole on the putting green is not a matter covered under the Rules of Golf. However, when setting such locations, various specific points should be considered.

Richie Ramsay's caddie looks on forlornly having infringed Rule 16-1 during the 2006 US Amateur Championship.

There must be sufficient putting surface between the hole and the front and the sides of the green to accommodate the required shot. For example, if the hole requires a long iron or wood shot to the green, the hole should be placed deeper in the green and farther from its sides than would be the case if the hole requires a short pitch shot.

It is recommended that the hole should be positioned at least four paces from any edge of the green. In addition, an area of 2–3 feet (0.6–0.9 metres) in radius around the hole should be as nearly level as possible. Every effort should be made to ensure that holes are not positioned within three paces of a very severe slope or ridge or of a recently used hole. In general, there should be a balanced selection of hole positions for the entire course with respect to left, right, central, front and back positions. Six quite difficult, six moderately difficult and six relatively easy positions are recommended. One should also try to keep a balance of using the left and right of the green: for example, on the first nine, there should be four hole positions to the left, four to the right and one in the centre. The second nine should be similar.

Finally, in order to observe the Rules of Golf, the greenkeeper who cuts the hole must make sure that any hole-liner does not exceed 4¼ inches (108 mm) in outer diameter, and if possible any liner must be sunk at least 1 inch (25.4 mm) below the putting green surface.

Additional guidance regarding hole positions is contained in The R&A's *Guidance on Running a Competition* publication (available via The R&A website, www.randa.org).

Q Why can't spike marks be repaired?
A The repair of spike marks that might assist the player in his subsequent play of the hole would constitute a breach of Rule 16-1c. It is not always possible to distinguish spike marks from other damage or irregularities of surface, so allowing the repair of spike marks would, in effect, entail permitting any damage or irregularity of surface on the putting green to be repaired. This is contrary to the fundamental principle of "playing the course as you find it" and it would undoubtedly lead to an increase in slow play as players attempt to perfect their line of putt.

RULE **17**

THE FLAGSTICK

Definitions   All defined terms are in *italics* and are listed alphabetically in the Definitions section – see pages 13–24.

17-1   **Flagstick Attended, Removed or Held Up**
Before making a *stroke* from anywhere on the *course*, the player may have the *flagstick* attended, removed or held up to indicate the position of the *hole*.

If the *flagstick* is not attended, removed or held up before the player makes a *stroke*, it must not be attended, removed or held up during the *stroke* or while the player's ball is in motion if doing so might influence the movement of the ball.

Note 1   If the *flagstick* is in the *hole* and anyone stands near it while a *stroke* is being made, he is deemed to be attending the *flagstick*.

Note 2   If, prior to the *stroke*, the *flagstick* is attended, removed or held up by anyone with the player's knowledge and he makes no objection, the player is deemed to have authorised it.

Note 3   If anyone attends or holds up the *flagstick* while a *stroke* is being made, he is deemed to be attending the *flagstick* until the ball comes to rest.
(Moving attended, removed or held up flagstick while ball in motion – see Rule 24-1.)

17-2   Unauthorised Attendance

If an opponent or his *caddie* in match play or a *fellow-competitor* or his *caddie* in stroke play, without the player's authority or prior knowledge, attends, removes or holds up the *flagstick* during the *stroke* or while the ball is in motion, and the act might influence the movement of the ball, the opponent or *fellow-competitor* incurs the applicable penalty.

Adjustment of flagstick: player's ball off green

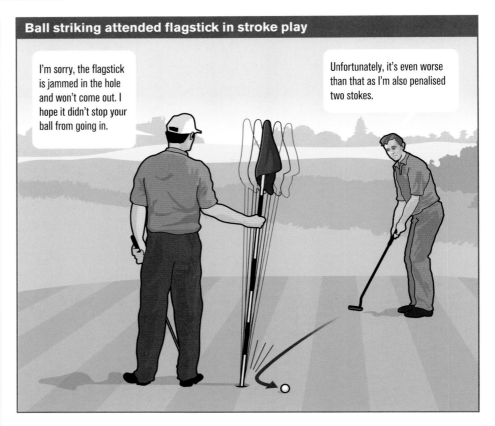

Ball striking attended flagstick in stroke play

I'm sorry, the flagstick is jammed in the hole and won't come out. I hope it didn't stop your ball from going in.

Unfortunately, it's even worse than that as I'm also penalised two stokes.

*Penalty

For breach of Rule 17-1 or 17-2:
Match play – Loss of hole; **Stroke play** – Two strokes.
*In stroke play, if a breach of Rule 17-2 occurs and the *competitor's* ball subsequently strikes the *flagstick*, the person attending or holding it or anything carried by him, the *competitor* incurs no penalty. The ball is played as it lies except that, if the *stroke* was made on the *putting green*, the *stroke* is cancelled and the ball must be replaced and replayed.

17-3 Ball Striking Flagstick or Attendant

The player's ball must not strike:
a. The *flagstick* when it is attended, removed or held up;
b. The person attending or holding up the *flagstick* or anything carried by him; or
c. The *flagstick* in the *hole*, unattended, when the *stroke* has been made on the *putting green*.

Exception

When the *flagstick* is attended, removed or held up without the player's authority – see Rule 17-2.

Penalty

For breach of Rule 17-3:
Match play – Loss of hole; **Stroke play** – Two strokes and the ball must be played as it lies.

Ball strikes flagstick lying on green in match play

17-4 **Ball Resting Against Flagstick**

When a player's ball rests against the *flagstick* in the *hole* and the ball is not *holed*, the player or another person authorised by him may move or remove the *flagstick*, and if the ball falls into the *hole*, the player is deemed to have *holed* out with his last *stroke*; otherwise, the ball, if *moved*, must be placed on the lip of the *hole*, without penalty.

RULE 17
INCIDENTS

During The 1995 Open at St. Andrews, Peter Fowler of Australia found himself on the front edge of the 2nd green of the Old Course, with the hole in the back left corner beyond the huge humps and swales that are a feature of the green. He asked the Referee if he could play the stroke with a wedge. The Rules do not stipulate that a player must use a putter when his ball is on the green and, therefore, he was given the go-ahead and pitched to within three feet of the hole.

Corey Pavin was on the other half of this double green, playing the 16th. He congratulated Fowler on a great shot, but warned, "Next time have the flag attended. It's a two-shot penalty if you hit the stick." The fact that the ball was on the green and, therefore, Rule 17-3c could have been breached, had escaped everyone else's attention.

The incident repeated itself in The 2000 Open at the same hole, this time with Jack Nicklaus. Nicklaus had hit his second shot well to the left, on the 16th-hole portion of the green, with a bunker between himself and the hole on the 2nd. He floated up a perfect wedge shot that almost went in the hole. The Referee accompanying the group was unsighted by the bunker and assumed that Nicklaus had played his shot from the fairway beyond the green.

As they walked to the next tee Nicklaus admitted that he was unsure if his ball was on the green or not and the Referee reminded him that if he had played from the green he should have had the flagstick attended.

"I had a 40-yard pitch shot over a bunker," said Nicklaus after the round. "You don't think much about having the pin attended. I've never done that before. It never entered my mind."

Another very uncommon incident in professional golf occurred with Phillip Price during the 2004 Dubai Desert Classic. Having played his second shot just on to the green at the par-5 3rd hole, his caddie was about to attend the flagstick prior to the Welshman putting. At this point, Price asked his caddie to take a look at the line of putt from behind his ball.

After conferring on the line, Price and his caddie forgot to have the flagstick attended and the player putted from the green with the flagstick in the hole, which, of itself, is not a breach of the Rules. Unfortunately, Price's putt was perfect and the ball rolled into the hole. Rule 17-3c provides that the player's ball must not strike the flagstick in the hole when a stroke has been made from the putting green and the resultant two-stroke penalty meant that Price's eagle three became a par 5.

In the 2007 Arnold Palmer Invitational, Boo Weekley found himself incurring a two-stroke penalty after trying to save his fellow-competitor, Tom Johnson, from a penalty during their third round.

At the par-3 2nd hole, Johnson hit his tee-shot on to the right side of the green and lay it 85 feet from the hole. Because of the steep slope on the green and the back-left hole location, he determined that the best way to get the ball close to the hole was to chip from the green, which is permitted, and try to land it in the back fringe so the ball could run down to the hole. However, as Johnson later said, "I spaced out and forgot to tell my caddie to attend the pin." Johnson played the perfect shot and the ball was rolling down slowly towards the hole when Weekley noticed that the ball might strike the flagstick in the hole. He therefore ran over and pulled the flagstick out.

Someone in the gallery mentioned what he had seen to a Rules official, and the matter was raised with the players in the scoring area before they returned their score cards. "They asked me if I had authorised Boo to pull the pin," Johnson said. "And I didn't." This meant that Weekley had removed the flagstick without authorisation while a ball was in motion. As the act could have influenced the movement of Johnson's ball, Weekley was subject to a penalty of two strokes under Rule 17-2.

Weekley, whose 67 was turned into a 69, was reported as having said, "Thanks, I learned something" to the Rules officials. Johnson said, "I just put my arm around him and told him he handles adversity better than anyone I've ever played with."

FAQ

Q. May the player have the flagstick attended even if his ball is not on the putting green?

A Yes. Rule 17-1 states that, before making a stroke from anywhere on the course, the player may have the flagstick attended, removed or held up.

Q May a player putt with one hand while holding the flagstick with the other?

A Yes, provided the flagstick has been removed from the hole and the ball therefore does not strike it. If the ball were to strike the flagstick, a breach of Rule 17-3a would occur. The player must not lean on the flagstick in order to steady himself whilst he putts, as that would be contrary to Rule 14-3, resulting in a penalty of disqualification.

RULE 18 BALL AT REST MOVED

Definitions
All defined terms are in *italics* and are listed alphabetically in the Definitions section – see pages 13–24.

18-1 By Outside Agency

If a ball at rest is *moved* by an *outside agency*, there is no penalty and the ball must be replaced.

Note
It is a question of fact whether a ball has been *moved* by an *outside agency*. In order to apply this Rule, it must be known or virtually certain that an *outside agency* has *moved* the ball. In the absence of such knowledge or certainty, the player must play the ball as it lies or, if the ball is not found, proceed under Rule 27-1.
(Player's ball at rest moved by another ball – see Rule 18-5)

18-2 By Player, Partner, Caddie or Equipment
18-2 a General

When a player's ball is *in play*, if:

(i) the player, his *partner* or either of their *caddies* lifts or *moves* it, touches it purposely (except with a club in the act of *addressing* it) or causes it to *move* except as permitted by a *Rule*, or

(ii) *equipment* of the player or his *partner* causes the ball to *move*,

the player incurs a penalty of one stroke. If the ball is *moved*, it must be replaced unless the movement of the ball occurs after the player has begun the *stroke* or the backward movement of the club for the *stroke* and the *stroke* is made.

Under the *Rules* there is no penalty if a player accidentally causes his ball to *move* in the following circumstances:

- In searching for a ball in a *hazard* covered by *loose impediments* or sand, for a ball in an *obstruction* or *abnormal ground condition* or for a ball believed to be in water in a *water hazard* – Rule 12-1

Ball at rest moved

By Outside Agency – no penalty and replace ball (Rule 18-1).

By Player, Partner, Caddie or Equipment – one-stroke penalty and replace ball (Rule 18-2a).

After Address – one-stroke penalty and replace ball (Rule 18-2b).

By Opponent, Caddie or Equipment Not During Search – opponent incurs one-stroke penalty and replace ball (Rule 18-3b).

By Opponent, Caddie or Equipment During Search – no penalty and replace ball (Rule 18-3a).

By Another Ball – replace moved ball (Rule 18-5).

By Fellow-Competitor, Caddie or Equipment – no penalty and replace ball (Rule18-4).

In Measuring – no penalty and replace ball (Rule 18-6).

- In repairing a *hole* plug or ball mark – Rule 16-1c
- In measuring – Rule 18-6
- In lifting a ball under a *Rule* – Rule 20-1
- In placing or replacing a ball under a *Rule* – Rule 20-3a
- In removing a *loose impediment* on the *putting green* – Rule 23-1
- In removing movable *obstructions* – Rule 24-1

18-2 b   **Ball Moving After Address**

If a player's *ball in play moves* after he has *addressed* it (other than as a result of a *stroke*), the player is deemed to have *moved* the ball and **incurs a penalty of one stroke**. The ball must be replaced, unless the movement of the ball occurs after the player has begun the *stroke* or the backward movement of the club for the *stroke* and the *stroke* is made.

18-3   By Opponent, Caddie or Equipment in Match Play

18-3 a   **During Search**

If, during search for a player's ball, an opponent, his *caddie* or his *equipment moves* the ball, touches it or causes it to *move*, there is no penalty. If the ball is *moved*, it must be replaced.

18-3 b   **Other Than During Search**

If, other than during search for a player's ball, an opponent, his *caddie* or his *equipment moves* the ball, touches it purposely or causes it to *move*, except as otherwise provided in the *Rules*, **the opponent incurs a penalty of one stroke**. If the ball is *moved*, it must be replaced.
(Playing a wrong ball – see Rule 15-3)
(Ball moved in measuring – see Rule 18-6)

18-4   By Fellow-Competitor, Caddie or Equipment in Stroke Play

If a *fellow-competitor*, his *caddie* or his *equipment moves* the player's ball, touches it or causes it to *move*, there is no penalty. If the ball is *moved*, it must be replaced.
(Playing a wrong ball – see Rule 15-3)

18-5   By Another Ball

If a *ball in play* and at rest is *moved* by another ball in motion after a *stroke*, the *moved* ball must be replaced.

18-6   Ball Moved in Measuring

If a ball or ball-marker is *moved* in measuring while proceeding under or in determining the application of a *Rule*, the ball or ball-marker must be replaced. There is no penalty, provided the movement of the ball or ball-marker is directly attributable to the specific act of measuring. Otherwise, the provisions of Rules 18-2a, 18-3b, or 18-4 apply.

*Penalty | **For breach of Rule:**
Match play – Loss of hole; **Stroke play** – Two strokes.
*If a player who is required to replace a ball fails to do so, or if he makes a *stroke* at a ball *substituted* under Rule 18 when such *substitution* is not permitted, he incurs the general penalty for breach of Rule 18, but there is no additional penalty under this Rule.

Note 1 | If a ball to be replaced under this Rule is not immediately recoverable, another ball may be *substituted*.

Note 2 | If the original lie of a ball to be placed or replaced has been altered, see Rule 20-3b.

Note 3 | If it is impossible to determine the spot on which a ball is to be placed, see Rule 20-3c.

RULE 18

INCIDENTS

On his final hole (the 9th hole of the course) of his second round in the 2006 WGC-Bridgestone Invitational, Tiger Woods' second shot struck a paved path and bounced over the clubhouse. The only area that was out of bounds at Firestone was the driving range – areas are only out of bounds if the Committee defines them as out of bounds, generally by reference to stakes, a fence, etc. (see Definition of "out of bounds").

Although it took more than five minutes to find Woods' ball, within five minutes of the search commencing the Rules officials determined, via eyewitness testimony, that it was virtually certain that someone had taken the ball. If an outside agency takes a ball, Rule 18-1 provides that another ball is replaced at the spot from which the original ball was moved, without penalty.

The final outcome was that Woods was permitted to drop a ball, without penalty, at the side of the clubhouse, because, at the spot where the ball lay before being moved by the outside agency, Woods would have had interference from the clubhouse and its parking area (a single immovable obstruction) and also from the grandstands behind the 9th green (a temporary immovable obstruction). Using the Local Rule for relief from temporary immovable obstructions, the Rules officials correctly permitted Woods to drop a ball at a position in which he no

Tiger Woods consults with Rules officials at the 2006 WGC-Bridgestone Invitational after hitting his ball over the clubhouse.

Angel Cabrera and a Rules official await a decision on his ball, which had rolled down the slight slope. Under Rule 18-2, if a ball is moved, it must be replaced unless the movement of the ball occurs after the player has begun the stroke.

longer had interference on his line of sight to the flagstick from the grandstands (see Appendix I for further information on the specimen Local Rule for temporary immovable obstructions).

Rule 18 was again infringed when a misunderstanding between Chris DiMarco and a Rules official at the 2006 HSBC Champions Tournament led to an unusual situation in which a score card was altered after it had been returned. On the first day, DiMarco was on the 8th green and had just grounded his putter behind the ball to tap in a short putt, when his ball moved. At that point, DiMarco called for a Rules official, and they agreed that, as the player had not completed his stance, and therefore had not addressed the ball, he was not automatically deemed to have caused the ball to move. The question then became whether the grounding of the club had caused the ball to move, in which case DiMarco would incur a one-stroke penalty under Rule 18-2a and the ball would be replaced.

Because the Rules official had misconstrued DiMarco's comments on how close his putter was to the ball when it was grounded, he ruled that the ball had moved of its own volition and DiMarco was advised to play the ball from its new position without penalty. However, on reviewing the incident on television later, it became clear to the Committee that the proximity of DiMarco's club to the ball when it was grounded was such that the weight of evidence was strongly in favour of the player's actions having caused the ball to move and that he should have been penalised.

By this point, DiMarco had returned his score card without a penalty included, but as the failure to include the penalty was due to the Rules official's instruction, based on a misunderstanding of the player's comments, it would have been unfair to disqualify the player for returning a score lower than actually taken. In such a case, Decision 34-3/1 allows for the correction of an incorrect decision, and in this case that meant adding a penalty stroke to the player's score for the hole. Although under Rule 18-2a the ball should have been replaced, it was too late to correct that error and no penalty was applied for the ball having been played from the wrong position in view of the Rules official's advice.

Decision 34-3/1 provides a necessary exception to the basic principle under Rule 6-6c – no alteration can be made on a score card once it is returned to the Committee by a competitor.

A Rules official was called during the final round of the 2006 BMW Championship at Wentworth and a discussion ensued about whether Angel Cabrera's actions of taking a practice swing had caused his ball to move or whether the ball had moved of its own volition. Cabrera had touched the ground with a practice swing quite near his ball, which was precariously balanced on a slight slope in the rough, and a few seconds later the ball had rolled off its spot and come to rest in another place.

If it was determined that the player had caused the ball to move, he would have been required to replace the ball under penalty of one stroke (Rule 18-2a). If the player had not caused the ball to move, there would be no penalty and the ball would be played from its new position.

In some cases, it may never be possible to say with absolute certainty what, in fact, has caused the ball to move. Decision 18-2a/30 provides that such decisions need to be made on the balance of the weight of evidence. On this basis, as the ball had been at rest for a considerable period of time prior to Cabrera making the practice swing and the movement of the ball had occurred so quickly after the practice swing had been made, it was ruled that the Argentine's actions had caused the ball to move and he incurred a one-stroke penalty under Rule 18-2a and replaced the ball.

RULE 19 BALL IN MOTION DEFLECTED OR STOPPED

Definitions All defined terms are in *italics* and are listed alphabetically in the Definitions section – see pages 13–24.

19-1 By Outside Agency

If a player's ball in motion is accidentally deflected or stopped by any *outside agency*, it is a *rub of the green*, there is no penalty and the ball must be played as it lies except:

a. If a player's ball in motion after a *stroke* other than on the *putting green* comes to rest in or on any moving or animate *outside agency*, the ball must *through the green* or in a *hazard* be dropped, or on the *putting green* be placed, as near as possible to the spot directly under the place where the ball came to rest in or on the *outside agency*, but not nearer the *hole*, and

b. If a player's ball in motion after a *stroke* on the *putting green* is deflected or stopped by, or comes to rest in or on, any moving or animate *outside agency*

Ball in motion deflected or stopped

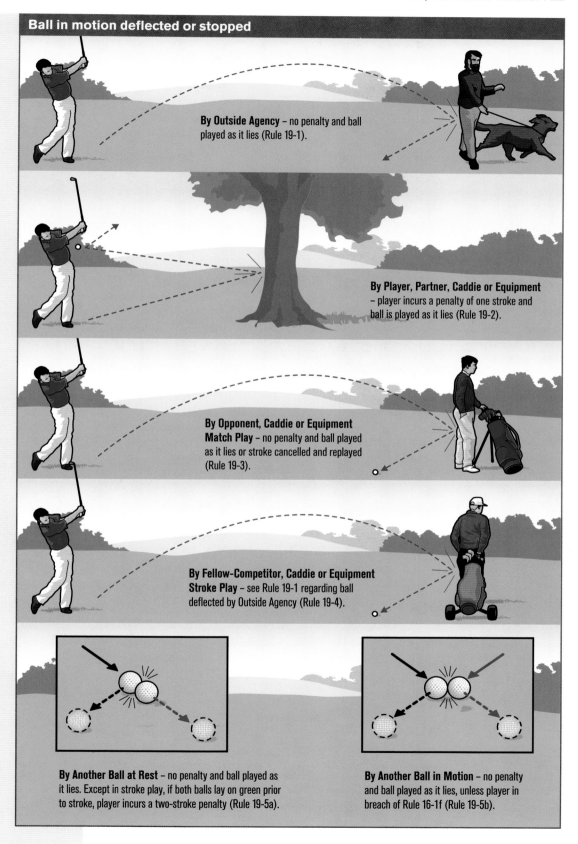

By Outside Agency – no penalty and ball played as it lies (Rule 19-1).

By Player, Partner, Caddie or Equipment – player incurs a penalty of one stroke and ball is played as it lies (Rule 19-2).

By Opponent, Caddie or Equipment Match Play – no penalty and ball played as it lies or stroke cancelled and replayed (Rule 19-3).

By Fellow-Competitor, Caddie or Equipment Stroke Play – see Rule 19-1 regarding ball deflected by Outside Agency (Rule 19-4).

By Another Ball at Rest – no penalty and ball played as it lies. Except in stroke play, if both balls lay on green prior to stroke, player incurs a two-stroke penalty (Rule 19-5a).

By Another Ball in Motion – no penalty and ball played as it lies, unless player in breach of Rule 16-1f (Rule 19-5b).

except a worm, insect or the like, the *stroke* is cancelled. The ball must be replaced and replayed.

If the ball is not immediately recoverable, another ball may be *substituted*.

Exception   Ball striking person attending or holding up *flagstick* or anything carried by him – see Rule 17-3b.

Note   If the *referee* or the *Committee* determines that a player's ball has been purposely deflected or stopped by an *outside agency*, Rule 1-4 applies to the player. If the *outside agency* is a *fellow-competitor* or his *caddie*, Rule 1-2 applies to the *fellow-competitor*. (Player's ball deflected or stopped by another ball – see Rule 19-5)

19-2   By Player, Partner, Caddie or Equipment

If a player's ball is accidentally deflected or stopped by himself, his *partner* or either of their *caddies* or *equipment*, **the player incurs a penalty of one stroke.** The ball must be played as it lies, except when it comes to rest in or on the player's, his *partner's* or either of their *caddies'* clothes or *equipment*, in which case the ball must *through the green* or in a *hazard* be dropped, or on the *putting green* be placed, as near as possible to the spot directly under the place where the ball came to rest in or on the article, but not nearer the *hole*.

Exceptions   1 Ball striking person attending or holding up flagstick or anything carried by him – see Rule 17-3b.
2 Dropped ball – see Rule 20-2a.
(Ball purposely deflected or stopped by player, partner or caddie – see Rule 1-2)

19-3   By Opponent, Caddie or Equipment in Match Play

If a player's ball is accidentally deflected or stopped by an opponent, his *caddie* or his *equipment*, there is no penalty. The player may, before another *stroke* is made by either *side*, cancel the *stroke* and play a ball, without penalty, as nearly as possible at the spot from which the original ball was last played (Rule 20-5) or he may play the ball as it lies. However, if the player elects not to cancel the *stroke* and the ball has come to rest in or on the opponent's or his *caddie's* clothes or *equipment*, the ball must *through the green* or in a *hazard* be dropped, or on the *putting green* be placed, as near as possible to the spot directly under the place where the ball came to rest in or on the article, but not nearer the *hole*.

Exception   Ball striking person attending or holding up *flagstick* or anything carried by him – see Rule 17-3b.
(Ball purposely deflected or stopped by opponent or caddie – see Rule 1-2)

19-4   By Fellow-Competitor, Caddie or Equipment in Stroke Play

See Rule 19-1 regarding ball deflected by *outside agency*.

Exception Ball striking person attending or holding up *flagstick* or anything carried by him – see Rule 17-3b.

19-5 By Another Ball

19-5 a **At Rest**

If a player's ball in motion after a *stroke* is deflected or stopped by a *ball in play* and at rest, the player must play his ball as it lies. In match play, there is no penalty. In stroke play, there is no penalty unless both balls lay on the *putting green* prior to the *stroke*, in which case **the player incurs a penalty of two strokes.**

19-5 b **In Motion**

If a player's ball in motion after a *stroke* is deflected or stopped by another ball in motion after a *stroke*, the player must play his ball as it lies. There is no penalty, unless the player was in breach of Rule 16-1f, in which case **he incurs the penalty for breach of that Rule**.

Exception If the player's ball is in motion after a *stroke* on the *putting green* and the other ball in motion is an *outside agency* – see Rule 19-1b.

Penalty **For breach of Rule:**
Match play – Loss of hole; **Stroke play** – Two strokes.

Tiger Woods' ball was deemed to have been deflected unintentionally when it went into the gallery lining the fairway at the 2006 PGA Championship, so Rule 19-1 was not invoked. However, subsequent camera evidence spotted that the ball had been deliberately deflected by a spectator.

RULE 19

INCIDENTS

Tiger Woods found himself in a situation involving Rule 19 at the 1st hole in the second round of the 2006 PGA Championship. Woods' drive went left towards the gallery lining the fairway. It bounced near a fairway bunker, was deflected by a spectator and came to rest near the rope line restricting the gallery. A Rules official in the area immediately asked for information – including whether or not the ball was purposefully or accidentally deflected – from spectators and marshals who were present. No one was of the opinion that the ball had been purposefully deflected and, therefore, it was correctly played as it lay.

It later came to light through the use of television replays that there had, in fact, been a deliberate deflection by one of the spectators, who had raised a hand and swatted the ball back towards the fairway, although the ball had deflected only far enough to come to rest in thick rough. Had this information been available to the officials at the time, under the Note to Rule 19-1 they could have taken the view that, without the deflection, the ball would have come to rest beyond the gallery in the area and, in equity (Rule 1-4), Woods would have been required to drop his ball at the spot where it was estimated that it would have come to rest without the deliberate spectator intervention.

In the course of the 2003 Masters Tournament, Jeff Maggert accidentally deflected his own ball in an attempt to play from the fairway bunker at the 3rd hole. Maggert was playing in the final group on the final day when his drive at the par-4 finished in one of four bunkers at the left of the landing zone. The ball was far enough behind the forward lip of the bunker for him to judge that he could play a full approach to the putting green. However, once struck, the ball smashed into the lip, ricocheted backwards and hit him. The Rules official walking with the group informed Maggert that a two-stroke penalty had been incurred and the ball had to be played as it lay (Rule 19-2b).

However, further to the introduction of the new Rules on 1 January 2008, if the same incident were to occur now the result would be a penalty of one stroke. This is due to the fact that the penalty for a player's ball in motion being accidentally deflected or stopped by himself, his partner or either of their caddies or equipment has been reduced from loss of hole in match play and two strokes in stroke play to one stroke in both forms of play.

If a player accidentally deflects his own ball, as Jeff Maggert did at the 2003 Masters, he is given a one-stroke penalty.

RULE 20 LIFTING, DROPPING AND PLACING; PLAYING FROM WRONG PLACE

Definitions All defined terms are in *italics* and are listed alphabetically in the Definitions section – see pages 13–24.

20-1 Lifting and Marking

A ball to be lifted under the *Rules* may be lifted by the player, his *partner* or another person authorised by the player. In any such case, the player is responsible for any breach of the *Rules*.

The position of the ball must be marked before it is lifted under a *Rule* that requires it to be replaced. If it is not marked, **the player incurs a penalty of one stroke** and the ball must be replaced. If it is not replaced, **the player incurs the general penalty for breach of this Rule** but there is no additional penalty under Rule 20-1.

If a ball or ball-marker is accidentally *moved* in the process of lifting the ball under a *Rule* or marking its position, the ball or ball-marker must be replaced. There is no penalty, provided the movement of the ball or ball-marker is directly attributable to the specific act of marking the position of or lifting the ball. Otherwise, **the player incurs a penalty of one stroke** under this Rule or Rule 18-2a.

Procedure for lifting ball

Although I want your ball lifted because it is interfering with my play, why are you marking it?

Because when a ball is lifted anywhere on the course and it has to be replaced, its position must be marked.

The player shall stand up straight, hold the ball at shoulder height and arm's length and drop it.

Exception If a player incurs a penalty for failing to act in accordance with Rule 5-3 or 12-2, there is no additional penalty under Rule 20-1.

Note The position of a ball to be lifted should be marked by placing a ball-marker, a small coin or other similar object immediately behind the ball. If the ball-marker interferes with the play, *stance* or *stroke* of another player, it should be placed one or more clubhead-lengths to one side.

20-2 Dropping and Re-Dropping

20-2 a **By Whom and How**

A ball to be dropped under the *Rules* must be dropped by the player himself. He must stand erect, hold the ball at shoulder height and arm's length and drop it. If a ball is dropped by any other person or in any other manner and the error is not corrected as provided in Rule 20-6, **the player incurs a penalty of one stroke**.

If the ball, when dropped, touches any person or the *equipment* of any player before or after it strikes a part of the *course* and before it comes to rest, the ball must be re-dropped, without penalty. There is no limit to the number of times a ball must be re-dropped in these circumstances.
(Taking action to influence position or movement of ball – see Rule 1-2)

20-2 b   **Where to Drop**

When a ball is to be dropped as near as possible to a specific spot, it must be dropped not nearer the *hole* than the specific spot which, if it is not precisely known to the player, must be estimated.

A ball when dropped must first strike a part of the *course* where the applicable *Rule* requires it to be dropped. If it is not so dropped, Rules 20-6 and 20-7 apply.

20-2 c   **When to Re-Drop**

A dropped ball must be re-dropped, without penalty, if it:

(i)   rolls into and comes to rest in a *hazard*;

(ii) rolls out of and comes to rest outside a *hazard*;

(iii) rolls onto and comes to rest on a *putting green*;

(iv) rolls and comes to rest *out of bounds*;

(v)   rolls to and comes to rest in a position where there is interference by the condition from which relief was taken under Rule 24-2b (immovable obstruction), Rule 25-1 (abnormal ground conditions), Rule 25-3 (wrong putting green) or a Local Rule (Rule 33-8a), or rolls back into the pitch-mark from which it was lifted under Rule 25-2 (embedded ball);

(vi) rolls and comes to rest more than two club-lengths from where it first struck a part of the *course*; or

page 103 of 192

(vii) rolls and comes to rest nearer the *hole* than:

(a) its original position or estimated position (see Rule 20-2b) unless otherwise permitted by the *Rules*; or

(b) the *nearest point of relief* or maximum available relief (Rule 24-2, 25-1 or 25-3); or

(c) the point where the original ball last crossed the margin of the *water hazard* or *lateral water hazard* (Rule 26-1).

If the ball when re-dropped rolls into any position listed above, it must be placed as near as possible to the spot where it first struck a part of the *course* when re-dropped.

Note 1   If a ball when dropped or re-dropped comes to rest and subsequently *moves*, the ball must be played as it lies, unless the provisions of any other *Rule* apply.

Note 2   If a ball to be re-dropped or placed under this Rule is not immediately recoverable, another ball may be *substituted*.
(Use of dropping zone – see Appendix I; Part B; section 8)

20-3   Placing and Replacing

20-3 a   By Whom and Where

A ball to be placed under the *Rules* must be placed by the player or his *partner*. If a ball is to be replaced, the player, his *partner* or the person who lifted or *moved* it must place it on the spot from which it was lifted or *moved*. If the ball is placed or replaced by any other person and the error is not corrected as provided in Rule 20-6, **the player incurs a penalty of one stroke**. In any such case, the player is responsible for any other breach of the *Rules* that occurs as a result of the placing or replacing of the ball.

If a ball or ball-marker is accidentally *moved* in the process of placing or replacing the ball, the ball or ball-marker must be replaced. There is no penalty, provided the movement of the ball or ball-marker is directly attributable to the specific act of placing or replacing the ball or removing the ball-marker. Otherwise, **the player incurs a penalty of one stroke** under Rule 18-2a or 20-1.

If a ball to be replaced is placed other than on the spot from which it was lifted or *moved* and the error is not corrected as provided in Rule 20-6, **the player incurs the general penalty, loss of hole in match play or two strokes in stroke play, for a breach of the applicable *Rule*.**

20-3 b   Lie of Ball to be Placed or Replaced Altered

If the original lie of a ball to be placed or replaced has been altered:
(i) except in a *hazard*, the ball must be placed in the nearest lie most similar to the original lie that is not more than one club-length from the original lie, not nearer the *hole* and not in a *hazard*;
(ii) in a *water hazard*, the ball must be placed in accordance with Clause (i) above, except that the ball must be placed in the *water hazard*;

(iii) in a *bunker*, the original lie must be re-created as nearly as possible and the ball must be placed in that lie.

20-3 c   **Spot Not Determinable**
If it is impossible to determine the spot where the ball is to be placed or replaced:
(i) *through the green*, the ball must be dropped as near as possible to the place where it lay but not in a *hazard* or on a *putting green*;
(ii) in a *hazard*, the ball must be dropped in the *hazard* as near as possible to the place where it lay;
(iii) on the *putting green*, the ball must be placed as near as possible to the place where it lay but not in a *hazard*.

Exception   When resuming play (Rule 6-8d), if the spot where the ball is to be placed is impossible to determine, it must be estimated and the ball placed on the estimated spot.

20-3 d   **Ball Fails to Come to Rest on Spot**
If a ball when placed fails to come to rest on the spot on which it was placed, there is no penalty and the ball must be replaced. If it still fails to come to rest on that spot:
(i) except in a *hazard*, it must be placed at the nearest spot where it can be placed at rest that is not nearer the *hole* and not in a *hazard*;
(ii) in a *hazard*, it must be placed in the *hazard* at the nearest spot where it can be placed at rest that is not nearer the *hole*.
If a ball when placed comes to rest on the spot on which it is placed, and it subsequently *moves*, there is no penalty and the ball must be played as it lies, unless the provisions of any other *Rule* apply.

Penalty For breach of Rule 20-1, 20-2 or 20-3:
Match play – Loss of hole; **Stroke play** – Two strokes.

20-4 When Ball Dropped or Placed is in Play

If the player's *ball in play* has been lifted, it is again in play when dropped or placed.

A *substituted ball* becomes the *ball in play* when it has been dropped or placed.
(Ball incorrectly substituted – see Rule 15-2)
(Lifting ball incorrectly substituted, dropped or placed – see Rule 20-6)

20-5 Making Next Stroke from Where Previous Stroke Made

When a player elects or is required to make his next *stroke* from where a previous *stroke* was made, he must proceed as follows:

(a) On the Teeing Ground: The ball to be played must be played from within the *teeing ground*. It may be played from anywhere within the *teeing ground* and may be teed.

(b) Through the Green: The ball to be played must be dropped and when dropped must first strike a part of the *course through the green*.

(c) In a Hazard: The ball to be played must be dropped and when dropped must first strike a part of the *course* in the *hazard*.

(d) On the Putting Green: The ball to be played must be placed on the *putting green*.

Lie of ball altered

Playing from the wrong place

If a player moves his ball-marker a putter head length to one side, he must remember to put it back before he putts. Otherwise, the player will be penalised for playing from a wrong place.

Penalty	**For breach of Rule 20-5:** **Match play** – Loss of hole; **Stroke play** – Two strokes.

20-6 Lifting Ball Incorrectly Substituted, Dropped or Placed

A ball incorrectly *substituted*, dropped or placed in a wrong place or otherwise not in accordance with the *Rules* but not played may be lifted, without penalty, and the player must then proceed correctly.

20-7 Playing from Wrong Place

20-7 a General

A player has played from a wrong place if he makes a *stroke* at his *ball in play*:
(i) on a part of the *course* where the *Rules* do not permit a *stroke* to be played or a ball to be dropped or placed; or
(ii) when the *Rules* require a dropped ball to be re-dropped or a *moved* ball to be replaced.

Note For a ball played from outside the *teeing ground* or from a wrong *teeing ground* – see Rule 11-4.

20-7 b Match Play

If a player makes a *stroke* from a wrong place, **he loses the hole**.

20-7 c

Stroke Play

If a *competitor* makes a *stroke* from a wrong place, **he incurs a penalty of two strokes under the applicable *Rule*.** He must play out the hole with the ball played from the wrong place, without correcting his error, provided he has not committed a serious breach (see Note 1).

If a *competitor* becomes aware that he has played from a wrong place and believes that he may have committed a serious breach, he must, before making a *stroke* on the next *teeing ground*, play out the hole with a second ball played in accordance with the *Rules*. If the hole being played is the last hole of the round, he must declare, before leaving the *putting green*, that he will play out the hole with a second ball played in accordance with the *Rules*.

If the *competitor* has played a second ball, he must report the facts to the *Committee* before returning his score card; if he fails to do so, **he is disqualified.** The *Committee* must determine whether the *competitor* has committed a serious breach of the applicable *Rule*. If he has, the score with the second ball counts and **the *competitor* must add two *penalty strokes*** to his score with that ball. If the *competitor* has committed a serious breach and has failed to correct it as outlined above, **he is disqualified.**

Note 1

A *competitor* is deemed to have committed a serious breach of the applicable *Rule* if the *Committee* considers he has gained a significant advantage as a result of playing from a wrong place.

Note 2

If a *competitor* plays a second ball under Rule 20-7c and it is ruled not to count, *strokes* made with that ball and *penalty strokes* incurred solely by playing that ball are disregarded. If the second ball is ruled to count, the *stroke* made from the wrong place and any *strokes* subsequently taken with the original ball including *penalty strokes* incurred solely by playing that ball are disregarded.

Note 3

If a player incurs a penalty for making a *stroke* from a wrong place, there is no additional penalty for *substituting* a ball when not permitted.

RULE **20**

INCIDENTS

Dropping the ball (under Rule 20) is one of the most fundamental and frequently used procedures in the Rules of Golf, and an excellent demonstration of the application of this Rule was seen during the closing holes of the 2004 MCI Heritage at Harbour Town Golf Links.

Ted Purdy was leading the tournament, but was acutely aware of a low total posted by eventual play-off winner Stewart Cink. At the 13th hole, Purdy's ball came to rest on a drain cover (an immovable obstruction) in the fairway, from which he was entitled to free relief. Purdy clearly knew the procedure under the relevant Rule (Rule 24-2) and decided to proceed without the assistance of an official. However, when he came to drop his ball within one club-length of the nearest point of relief, he did so with his hand well below shoulder height when the ball was released.

Rule 20-2a provides that a player, when dropping a ball, must stand erect, hold the ball at shoulder height and arm's length and drop it. If a player makes a stroke at a ball dropped in an incorrect manner, he is subject to a penalty of one stroke. However, if the error is realised prior to a stroke being made, it can be corrected without penalty by lifting the ball and dropping it correctly.

In Purdy's case, he was lucky that a Rules official was watching his procedure and intervened before the player made a stroke. It is the Rules official's duty to prevent a breach if he can do so. He advised Purdy of his error and had the player lift the ball and drop it properly, thus saving him a penalty stroke.

Less fortunate was Retief Goosen in the first round of the 2006 South African Airways Open. As he stood on the 17th tee, he was eight under par and could not have imagined what was about to happen on the 543-yard par 5. Having struck a wayward tee-shot, he then hit a poor provisional ball from the tee. Because he was unable to find his first ball within the five-minute search period, his provisional ball, which had been found in a bush, became the ball in play.

The South African elected to deem the provisional ball unplayable and (under Rule 28c) dropped within two club-lengths of the spot where the ball lay. The ball when dropped rolled outside the two club-length dropping area, but did not roll more than two club-lengths from where it had first struck the course and did not roll closer to the hole than the ball's original position. As the ball had not rolled into any of the positions requiring a re-drop under Rule 20-2c, the ball was in play.

Inexplicably, Goosen thought he had to re-drop because the ball had rolled outside the area measured under Rule 28c. He therefore lifted the ball, dropped it again and played from the new spot. As a result, he incurred the general penalty of two strokes under Rule 18 for lifting a ball without authority and failing to replace it. He later told officials that he knew the Rule but had just had a "brain freeze".

With a lost ball, an unplayable drop and two-stroke penalty, Goosen finished with an 11 on the 17th hole, although he still managed to birdie the final hole of the round to post a three-under-par 69.

Ian Woosnam failed to complete his first round in the 2004 Linde German Masters when he became frustrated by a lateral water hazard near the 9th green (his 18th hole).

In taking relief under penalty of one stroke, the Welshman dropped within two club-lengths of where the ball last crossed the margin of the hazard in accordance with Rule 26-1c, but the ball rolled back into the hazard. As required by Rule 20-2c, the player tried the drop a second time, but the same thing happened. Woosnam then placed the ball at rest on the spot where it first struck the ground after the second drop and walked forward to assess the next shot.

When Woosnam was walking back towards his ball, which was lying on a tightly cut slope, he saw it leave its position and roll back into the hazard. Rule 20-3d provides that, when a ball is placed at rest, it is in play and if it subsequently moves, there is no penalty, but the ball is in play at its new position. Unfortunately for the player, the new position was back in the lateral water hazard.

At this stage, Woosnam could have taken relief again under Rule 26-1, using the new point where the ball last crossed the margin of the hazard as a reference point. Rule 26-1a would also have allowed a return to where the last stroke was played from, thereby avoiding the sloping bank of the hazard. However, Woosnam elected to play the ball as it lay in the water and, after failing to get the ball out of the water with two swipes, he decided that enough was enough and headed for the clubhouse.

Even after the two attempts from the water, Woosnam could still have taken relief outside the hazard under Rule 26-2a, which essentially provides the player with the same relief options that were available prior to making the strokes in the hazard, but the player said later that he "wasn't in the mood to carry on".

"I hit my second shot into the water, dropped out under penalty at the nearest point of relief and walked away to view the shot. In that time the ball rolled back into the water and I faced another shot penalty. There was no chance of replacing the ball – I either had to play it as it lay or take the penalty."

FAQ

Q Must a player use a small coin or similar object to mark the position of his ball before lifting it?

A The Note to Rule 20-1 states in part that the position of the ball should be marked by placing a ball-marker, small coin or other small object immediately behind the ball. When the word "should" is used in the Rules of Golf it is a recommendation only and failure to comply does not result in a penalty – see the section entitled "How to Use the Rule Book" on page 6. The intention is to emphasise that use of a ball-marker or other small object (such as a coin) is considered to be the best way to mark a ball.

Q Is the person who lifted the player's ball the only person who may replace it?

A No. Up to a maximum of three different people may replace a ball, depending on the circumstances, that is the player, his partner or the person who lifted it. For example, in a four-ball match, if a player were to authorise his caddie to lift his ball, the caddie, the player or the player's partner could replace it. However, if the player lifts the ball himself, only the player or his partner may replace it – see Rule 20-3a.

RULE 21

CLEANING BALL

Definitions All defined terms are in *italics* and are listed alphabetically in the Definitions section – see pages 13–24.

A ball on the *putting green* may be cleaned when lifted under Rule 16-1b. Elsewhere, a ball may be cleaned when lifted, except when it has been lifted:
a. To determine if it is unfit for play (Rule 5-3);
b. For identification (Rule 12-2), in which case it may be cleaned only to the extent necessary for identification; or

c. Because it is assisting or interfering with play (Rule 22).

If a player cleans his ball during play of a hole except as provided in this Rule, **he incurs a penalty of one stroke** and the ball, if lifted, must be replaced.

If a player who is required to replace a ball fails to do so, he incurs the general penalty under the applicable Rule, but there is no additional penalty under Rule 21.

Exception   If a player incurs a penalty for failing to act in accordance with Rule 5-3, 12-2 or 22, there is no additional penalty under Rule 21.

RULE 22 BALL ASSISTING OR INTERFERING WITH PLAY

Definitions   All defined terms are in *italics* and are listed alphabetically in the Definitions section – see pages 13–24.

22-1   Ball Assisting Play

Except when a ball is in motion, if a player considers that a ball might assist any other player, he may:
a. Lift the ball if it is his ball; or
b. Have any other ball lifted.
A ball lifted under this Rule must be replaced (see Rule 20-3). The ball must not be cleaned unless it lies on the *putting green* (see Rule 21).

Ball interfering with or assisting play

As we're playing a match, I would like you to leave your ball where it is.

I'm sorry, but I'm entitled to mark and lift my ball and I'm going to do so.

In stroke play, a player required to lift his ball may play first rather than lift the ball.

In stroke play, if the *Committee* determines that *competitors* have agreed not to lift a ball that might assist any *competitor*, **they are disqualified**.

22-2 Ball Interfering with Play

Except when a ball is in motion, if a player considers that another ball might interfere with his play, he may have it lifted.

A ball lifted under this Rule must be replaced (see Rule 20-3). The ball must not be cleaned, unless it lies on the *putting green* (see Rule 21).

In stroke play, a player required to lift his ball may play first rather than lift the ball.

Note
Except on the *putting green*, a player may not lift his ball solely because he considers that it might interfere with the play of another player. If a player lifts his ball without being asked to do so, **he incurs a penalty of one stroke** for a breach of Rule 18-2a, but there is no additional penalty under Rule 22.

Penalty
For breach of Rule:
Match play – Loss of hole; **Stroke play** – Two strokes.

RULE 22

INCIDENTS

Because golf is played on the largest playing field of any sport, it's rare for one ball to touch another.

However, Jesper Parnevik and Scott Hoch found themselves in such a predicament just off the 6th green at Pinehurst No.2 during the 1999 US Open. Fortunately, the procedure in such a situation is concise.

Rule 22 allows any player to lift his ball if he believes it will assist another player, or have any ball lifted that might interfere with his play or assist any other player. Except on the putting green, a ball lifted under this Rule may not be cleaned.

Hoch and Parnevik both played just to the left side of the green at this 222-yard par 3. Upon arriving at the green, they found that the balls were touching one another and lay about three inches off the fringe in the Bermuda grass rough. Both balls were held slightly off the ground by the stiff nature of the grass. Because Hoch's ball was closer to the hole, it was necessary that it be lifted in order for Parnevik to play his shot.

When Hoch lifted his ball, Parnevik's moved an inch closer to the hole. Under a Rules official's watchful eye, Parnevik attempted to replace his ball in its original location. However, the supporting nature of the Bermuda grass could not be reintroduced and Parnevik's ball sunk a little deeper into the rough than its original position. Under the Rules, it does not matter if the movement is vertical or horizontal. The ball could not be replaced in its original position so that it would remain at rest.

A player is entitled to remove any loose impediment without penalty, except when both the loose impediment and the ball lie in or touch the same hazard.

Rule 20-3d covers such a situation by stating that if a ball, when placed or replaced, fails to come to rest on that spot it must be replaced. If it again fails to remain at rest, it must be placed at the nearest spot where it can be placed at rest, which is not nearer the hole and not in a hazard.

Therefore, Parnevik found another spot that was nearest to the original position where the ball would remain at rest. He chipped on to the green and in doing so altered Hoch's lie.

In this case, Hoch was entitled to the lie that his shot gave him. Since his lie had been altered, he found the nearest lie most similar to and within one club-length of his original lie and placed his ball at that spot. Then he chipped the ball in for a birdie two.

RULE 23 LOOSE IMPEDIMENTS

Definitions   All defined terms are in *italics* and are listed alphabetically in the Definitions section – see pages 13–24.

23-1   **Relief**
Except when both the *loose impediment* and the ball lie in or touch the same *hazard*, any *loose impediment* may be removed without penalty.

113

If the ball lies anywhere other than on the *putting green* and the removal of a *loose impediment* by the player causes the ball to *move*, Rule 18-2a applies.

On the *putting green*, if the ball or ball-marker is accidentally *moved* in the process of the player removing a *loose impediment*, the ball or ball-marker must be replaced. There is no penalty, provided the movement of the ball or ball-marker is directly attributable to the removal of the *loose impediment*. Otherwise, if the player causes the ball to *move*, **he incurs a penalty of one stroke** under Rule 18-2a.

When a ball is in motion, a *loose impediment* that might influence the movement of the ball must not be removed.

Note   If the ball lies in a *hazard*, the player must not touch or move any *loose impediment* lying in or touching the same *hazard* – see Rule 13-4c.

Penalty   **For breach of Rule:**
Match play – Loss of hole; **Stroke play** – Two strokes.
(Searching for ball in hazard – see Rule 12-1)
(Touching line of putt – see Rule 16-1a)

RULE 23
INCIDENTS

The Rules of Golf permitted Tiger Woods to gain assistance from his substantial gallery in moving a loose impediment during the 1999 Phoenix Open.

During the final round, Woods' drive from the 13th tee travelled 360 yards before finishing in the desert just off the left side of the fairway. The ball stopped about two feet directly behind a boulder that was roughly four feet wide, two feet high and two feet thick. The rock was too heavy for Woods to move by himself,

Loose impediments are natural objects that come in all shapes and sizes. At the 1999 Phoenix Open, Tiger Woods learned that a player can receive assistance in removing a large loose impediment. Details of this incident can be reviewed above.

and his ball was too close to it to play over or around. Without moving the rock, his best option would have been to play sideways onto the fairway.

With 225 yards to the putting green, Woods was not inclined to pitch out without first knowing what his options were with regard to the rock.

A PGA Tour Rules official appeared at the scene. With a glimmer of a smile on his face, Woods kicked the rock and asked, "... It's not a pebble but is it a loose impediment?"

The definition within the Rules of Golf states that loose impediments are natural objects that are not fixed or growing, not solidly embedded and do not adhere to the ball. There is no reference to size or weight.

Decision 23-1/2 states that stones of any size are loose impediments and may be removed, as long as they are not solidly embedded and their removal does not unduly delay play.

The official replied, "It's readily movable if you have people who can move it real quick."

"Really?" Woods responded to the revelation quietly.

Then the official added in an enquiring tone, "But it kind of looks embedded to me."

"It's embedded?" Woods asked as they both stepped back to look.

The official decided the stone was just lying on the desert floor and was not solidly embedded. He also knew that Decision 23-1/3 specifically permits spectators, caddies, fellow-competitors, essentially anyone, to assist in removing a large loose impediment.

Several men rolled the stone out of Woods' line of play as others watched and cheered. Following the removal, Woods shook each man's hand and then played his shot directly toward the green, where it finished in the bunker to the right of the green.

RULE 24 OBSTRUCTIONS

Definitions All defined terms are in *italics* and are listed alphabetically in the Definitions section – see pages 13–24.

24-1 ### Movable Obstruction
A player may take relief, without penalty, from a movable *obstruction* as follows:
a. If the ball does not lie in or on the *obstruction*, the *obstruction* may be removed. If the ball *moves*, it must be replaced, and there is no penalty, provided that the movement of the ball is directly attributable to the removal of the *obstruction*. Otherwise, Rule 18-2a applies.
b. If the ball lies in or on the *obstruction*, the ball may be lifted and the *obstruction* removed. The ball must *through the green* or in a *hazard* be

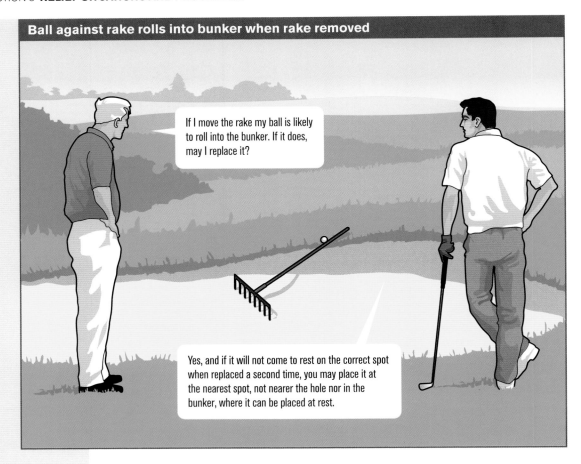

dropped, or on the *putting green* be placed, as near as possible to the spot directly under the place where the ball lay in or on the *obstruction*, but not nearer the *hole*.

The ball may be cleaned when lifted under this Rule.

When a ball is in motion, an *obstruction* that might influence the movement of the ball, other than *equipment* of any player or the *flagstick* when attended, removed or held up, must not be moved.

(Exerting influence on ball – see Rule 1-2)

Note   If a ball to be dropped or placed under this Rule is not immediately recoverable, another ball may be *substituted*.

24-2   Immovable Obstruction

24-2 a   Interference

Interference by an immovable *obstruction* occurs when a ball lies in or on the *obstruction*, or when the *obstruction* interferes with the player's *stance* or the area of his intended swing. If the player's ball lies on the *putting green*, interference also occurs if an immovable *obstruction* on the *putting green* intervenes on his *line of putt*. Otherwise, intervention on the *line of play* is not, of itself, interference under this Rule.

Flagstick removed when ball in motion

When a ball is in motion it is permissible to move a flagstick that has been removed and that might influence the movement of the ball.

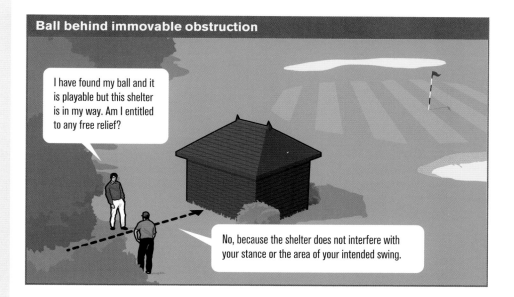

Ball behind immovable obstruction

I have found my ball and it is playable but this shelter is in my way. Am I entitled to any free relief?

No, because the shelter does not interfere with your stance or the area of your intended swing.

24-2 b   **Relief**

Except when the ball is in a *water hazard* or a *lateral water hazard*, a player may take relief from interference by an immovable *obstruction* as follows:

(i) Through the Green: If the ball lies *through the green*, the player must lift the ball and drop it, without penalty, within one club-length of and not nearer the *hole* than the *nearest point of relief*. The *nearest point of relief* must not be in a *hazard* or on a *putting green*. When the ball is dropped within one club-length of the *nearest point of relief*, the ball must first strike a part of the *course* at a spot that avoids interference by the immovable *obstruction* and is not in a *hazard* and not on a *putting green*.

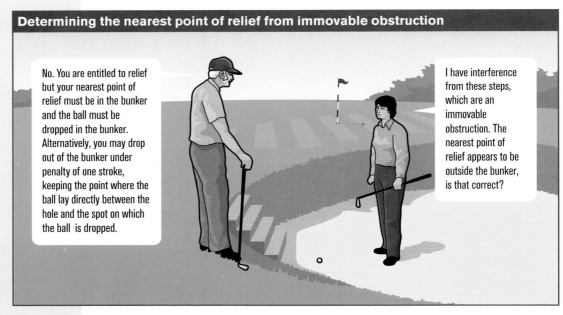

(ii) In a Bunker: If the ball is in a *bunker*, the player must lift the ball and drop it either:

(a) Without penalty, in accordance with Clause (i) above, except that the *nearest point of relief* must be in the *bunker* and the ball must be dropped in the *bunker*; or

(b) Under penalty of one stroke, outside the *bunker* keeping the point where the ball lay directly between the *hole* and the spot on which the ball is dropped, with no limit to how far behind the *bunker* the ball may be dropped.

(iii) On the Putting Green: If the ball lies on the *putting green*, the player must lift the ball and place it, without penalty, at the *nearest point of relief* that is not in a *hazard*. The *nearest point of relief* may be off the *putting green*.

(iv) On the Teeing Ground: If the ball lies on the *teeing ground*, the player must lift the ball and drop it, without penalty, in accordance with Clause (i) above.

The ball may be cleaned when lifted under this Rule.

(Ball rolling to a position where there is interference by the condition from which relief was taken – see Rule 20-2c(v))

Exception   A player may not take relief under this Rule if (**a**) it is clearly unreasonable for him to make a *stroke* because of interference by anything other than an immovable *obstruction* or (**b**) interference by an immovable *obstruction* would occur only through use of an unnecessarily abnormal *stance*, swing or direction of play.

Note 1   If a ball is in a *water hazard* (including a *lateral water hazard*), the player may not take relief from interference by an immovable *obstruction*. The player must play the ball as it lies or proceed under Rule 26-1.

Note 2   If a ball to be dropped or placed under this Rule is not immediately recoverable, another ball may be *substituted*.

Note 3   The *Committee* may make a Local Rule stating that the player must determine the *nearest point of relief* without crossing over, through or under the *obstruction*.

After David Frost was denied relief from the road to the left of the 2nd hole at Carnoustie he played his ball on to the road and then took relief under Rule 24-2 – see incident on pages 123–124.

24-3 Ball in Obstruction Not Found

It is a question of fact whether a ball that has not been found after having been struck toward an *obstruction* is in the *obstruction*. In order to apply this Rule, it must be known or virtually certain that the ball is in the *obstruction*. In the absence of such knowledge or certainty, the player must proceed under Rule 27-1.

24-3 a Ball in Movable Obstruction Not Found

If it is known or virtually certain that a ball that has not been found is in a movable *obstruction*, the player may *substitute* another ball and take relief,

No relief without penalty in water hazard

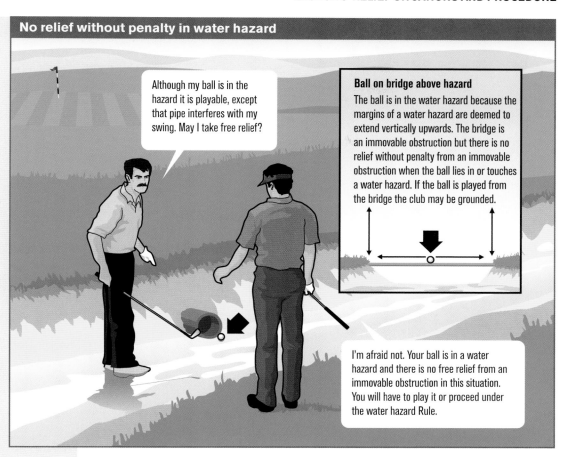

Although my ball is in the hazard it is playable, except that pipe interferes with my swing. May I take free relief?

Ball on bridge above hazard
The ball is in the water hazard because the margins of a water hazard are deemed to extend vertically upwards. The bridge is an immovable obstruction but there is no relief without penalty from an immovable obstruction when the ball lies in or touches a water hazard. If the ball is played from the bridge the club may be grounded.

I'm afraid not. Your ball is in a water hazard and there is no free relief from an immovable obstruction in this situation. You will have to play it or proceed under the water hazard Rule.

Stile in boundary fence

The stile interferes with my follow-through. May I obtain free relief?

Yes. The out-of-bounds fence is not an immovable obstruction, but the stile is.

without penalty, under this Rule. If he elects to do so, he must remove the *obstruction* and *through the green* or in a *hazard* drop a ball, or on the *putting green* place a ball, as near as possible to the spot directly under the place where the ball last crossed the outermost limits of the movable *obstruction*, but not nearer the hole.

24-3 b **Ball in Immovable Obstruction Not Found**

If it is known or virtually certain that a ball that has not been found is in an immovable *obstruction*, the player may take relief under this Rule. If he elects to do so, the spot where the ball last crossed the outermost limits of the *obstruction* must be determined and, for the purpose of applying this Rule, the ball is deemed to lie at this spot and the player must proceed as follows:

(i) Through the Green: If the ball last crossed the outermost limits of the immovable *obstruction* at a spot *through the green*, the player may *substitute* another ball, without penalty, and take relief as prescribed in Rule 24-2b(i).

(ii) In a Bunker: If the ball last crossed the outermost limits of the immovable *obstruction* at a spot in a *bunker*, the player may *substitute* another ball, without penalty, and take relief as prescribed in Rule 24-2b(ii).

(iii) In a Water Hazard (including a Lateral Water Hazard): If the ball last crossed the outermost limits of the immovable *obstruction* at a spot in a *water hazard*, the player is not entitled to relief without penalty. The player must proceed under Rule 26-1.

(iv) On the Putting Green: If the ball last crossed the outermost limits of the immovable *obstruction* at a spot on the *putting green*, the player may *substitute* another ball, without penalty, and take relief as prescribed in Rule 24-2b(iii).

Penalty **For breach of Rule:**
Match play – Loss of hole; **Stroke play** – Two strokes.

RULE 24

INCIDENTS

Since 1744, the basic tenets of the Rules have been to play the course as you find it, the ball as it lies and, if you are unsure of the proper procedure, to do what is fair. Harry Bradshaw held true to this spirit at the 1949 Open Championship.

Having shot a stunning first round 68 over Royal St George's, Bradshaw was tied with Roberto De Vicenzo one stroke behind Jimmy Adams. However, playing the 5th hole during the second round, Bradshaw's ball rolled into a discarded beer bottle from which the neck had been broken.

Rather than requesting a ruling for the relief to which he was entitled, Bradshaw determined on his own that he must play the ball as it lay. He took out his sand wedge and made a swing, which shattered the bottle and moved the ball slightly forward. He took a double bogey six.

The result of his playing out of this movable obstruction was that Bradshaw ultimately tied Bobby Locke of South Africa at 283. In the resulting 36-hole play-off, Locke scored 136 to Bradshaw's 147, to win the first of Locke's four Open Championship tournaments.

Under Rule 24-1, because Bradshaw's ball was in a movable obstruction, the ball could have been lifted and cleaned without penalty, the bottle removed and the ball dropped as nearly as possible to the spot directly under the place where the ball lay when it was in the bottle.

In choosing to take relief from an immovable obstruction, the ball must be dropped in a place that avoids interference by the immovable obstruction. Full relief must be taken. Payne Stewart learned this lesson in 1993 during the PGA Tour's annual stop in San Diego.

In taking relief from a cart path, Stewart dropped his ball in a place where, after taking his stance, the heel of his right shoe was still on the cart path from which he was taking relief. The television broadcast showed the breach clearly and Stewart was penalised two strokes for not taking complete relief from the immovable obstruction.

The Exception to Rule 24-2 states clearly that a player may not obtain relief under this Rule if interference would only occur through the use of an abnormal stance, swing or direction of play. This is one of the situations in the Rules where a Referee's judgement is called upon, as David Frost learned during the final round of the 1999 Open Championship at Carnoustie.

Harry Bradshaw views with disbelief his ball, which has rolled into a broken beer bottle.

Because Nick Dougherty's ball was lying just in front of some sleepers outside the bunker, he was instructed to drop the ball within one club-length of his nearest relief spot, under Rule 24-2b(i).

Playing with Justin Leonard in the penultimate group, Frost's drive at the 2nd hole was a low hook into the high rough. Near the area where he would stand to play the ball was a road. Frost argued to the attending Rules official that in order to play the ball, which was below his feet, he would have to widen his stance to such an extent that he would be standing on the road and, therefore, he was entitled to relief from an immovable obstruction.

The Referee did not accept the argument and told Frost that such play was not reasonable. It was the official's judgement that had the road not been there, Frost would not have used a stance that would place his left foot on the road. With the final pairing waiting on the tee, time ticked away as confirmation of the official's decision was requested over the radio. It was deemed final, and Frost played the ball as it lay. His shot from this awkward lie came to rest on the road, from where he was then granted relief under Rule 24-2.

In such a situation, the Rules official must consider how the player would attempt the shot if the obstruction in question were not present. In a stroke-play situation such as this one, the Rules are there to protect the field and prevent an unfair advantage of one player over all the others.

When the Committee declares an obstruction an integral part of the golf course, it eliminates any argument because there is no free relief. The most famous example of this is on the Road Hole at the Old Course in St Andrews. When a ball lies on the road immediately to the right of the green, it must be played as it lies. As the name of the hole suggests, the road has always been the most important element of the 17th hole and to allow relief would eliminate one of its essential obstacles. Thus, it is an integral part of the golf course.

At the 2005 Caltex Masters in Singapore, the eventual winner, Nick Dougherty, benefited from a ruling at the 16th hole on the final day, while leading the tournament by a single stroke from Colin Montgomerie.

Dougherty's tee-shot was pulled to the left and it appeared to have come to rest in a bunker with a large, sleepered face made out of thick wooden planks. However, the Definition of "Bunker" in the Rules of Golf provides that any grass-covered ground bordering or within a bunker is not part of the bunker and what had happened was that the player's ball had run through the bunker and come to rest on grass-covered ground just in front of the sleepers.

The sleepers themselves were immovable obstructions and, if Dougherty's ball had been in the bunker, his only options would have been to take relief in the bunker without penalty or drop outside the bunker, back on a line with the flagstick, under penalty of one stroke (Rule 24-2b(ii)). As it was, with the ball lying just outside the bunker, Rule 24-2b(i) allowed Dougherty to ascertain his nearest point of relief from the sleepers outside the bunker and then drop within one club-length of that spot not nearer to the hole. The drop put him in a much more favourable position, as sometimes occurs in free-relief situations, and he then played a superb shot to within three feet of the hole.

Dougherty commented, "I enjoyed a bit of good fortune with the drop, but the shot I played then was the most important of my career so far. I hit a class shot that pitched exactly where I wanted and the ball rolled close to the hole. I felt that shot gave me a valuable psychological edge, with Monty breathing down my neck."

FAQ

Q Should rakes be placed inside or outside bunkers?

A It is recommended that rakes be placed outside bunkers as, on balance, it is felt there is less likelihood of an advantage or disadvantage to the player.

In practice, players who leave rakes in bunkers frequently place them at the side, which tends to stop a ball rolling into the flat part of the bunker, resulting in a much more difficult shot than would otherwise have been the case. This is especially true of small bunkers.

If a ball comes to rest against a rake in the bunker, the player may proceed under Rule 24-1 (Movable Obstruction). However, it may not be possible to replace the ball on the same spot or find a spot in the bunker that is not nearer the hole.

If a rake is left in the middle of the bunker, the only way to get it there is to throw it into the bunker, thus damaging the surface. Also, if a rake is in the middle of a large bunker it is either not used or the player is obliged to rake a large area of the bunker resulting in unnecessary delay. Therefore, after considering all these aspects, it is recommended that rakes should be left outside bunkers in areas where they are least likely to affect the movement of the ball.

Q May stakes defining a water hazard or lateral water hazard be moved?

A A water hazard stake is an obstruction – see Definition of "obstruction". Consequently, if such a stake is movable, it may be removed without penalty, in accordance with Rule 24-1. A player may remove a movable obstruction anywhere on the course, irrespective of whether his ball lies in a water hazard or not.

25
ABNORMAL GROUND CONDITIONS, EMBEDDED BALL AND WRONG PUTTING GREEN

Definitions All defined terms are in *italics* and are listed alphabetically in the Definitions section – see pages 13–24.

25-1   Abnormal Ground Conditions

25-1 a   Interference

Interference by an *abnormal ground condition* occurs when a ball lies in or touches the condition or when the condition interferes with the player's *stance* or the area of his intended swing. If the player's ball lies on the *putting green*, interference also occurs if an *abnormal ground condition* on the *putting green* intervenes on his *line of putt*. Otherwise, intervention on the *line of play* is not, of itself, interference under this Rule.

Note The *Committee* may make a Local Rule stating that interference by an *abnormal ground condition* with a player's *stance* is deemed not to be, of itself, interference under this Rule.

25-1 b   Relief

Except when the ball is in a *water hazard* or a *lateral water hazard*, a player may take relief from interference by an *abnormal ground condition* as follows:

A fallen tree still attached to its stump is not ground under repair, but it can be so declared by the Committee.

A rut made by a tractor is not ground under repair, but the Committee would be justified in declaring a deep rut to be ground under repair.

Areas requiring preservation

If there is an area of the course, such as a plantation of young trees, which requires preservation the Committee should declare it "Ground Under Repair – Play Prohibited".

(i) Through the Green: If the ball lies *through the green*, the player must lift the ball and drop it, without penalty, within one club-length of and not nearer the *hole* than the *nearest point of relief*. The *nearest point of relief* must not be in a *hazard* or on a *putting green*. When the ball is dropped within one club-length of the *nearest point of relief*, the ball must first strike a part of the *course* at a spot that avoids interference by the condition and is not in a *hazard* and not on a *putting green*.

(ii) In a Bunker: If the ball is in a *bunker*, the player must lift the ball and drop it either:

(a) Without penalty, in accordance with Clause (i) above, except that the *nearest point of relief* must be in the *bunker* and the ball must be dropped in the *bunker* or, if complete relief is impossible, as near as possible to the spot where the ball lay, but not nearer the *hole*, on a part of the *course* in the *bunker* that affords maximum available relief from the condition; or

(b) Under penalty of one stroke, outside the *bunker* keeping the point where the ball lay directly between the *hole* and the spot on which the ball is dropped, with no limit to how far behind the *bunker* the ball may be dropped.

(iii) On the Putting Green: If the ball lies on the *putting green*, the player must lift the ball and place it, without penalty, at the *nearest point of relief* that is not in a *hazard* or, if complete relief is impossible, at the nearest position to where it lay that affords maximum available relief from the condition, but not nearer the *hole* and not in a *hazard*. The *nearest point of relief* or maximum available relief may be off the *putting green*.

(iv) On the Teeing Ground: If the ball lies on the *teeing ground*, the player must lift the ball and drop it, without penalty, in accordance with Clause (i) above.

The ball may be cleaned when lifted under Rule 25-1b.

(Ball rolling to a position where there is interference by the condition from which relief was taken – see Rule 20-2c(v))

Exception A player may not take relief under this Rule if (a) it is clearly unreasonable for him to make a *stroke* because of interference by anything other than an *abnormal ground condition* or (b) interference by an *abnormal ground condition* would occur only through use of an unnecessarily abnormal *stance*, swing or direction of play.

Note 1 If a ball is in a *water hazard* (including a *lateral water hazard*), the player is not entitled to relief, without penalty, from interference by an *abnormal ground condition*. The player must play the ball as it lies (unless prohibited by Local Rule) or proceed under Rule 26-1.

Note 2 If a ball to be dropped or placed under this Rule is not immediately recoverable, another ball may be *substituted*.

25-1 c **Ball in Abnormal Ground Condition Not Found**
It is a question of fact whether a ball that has not been found after having been struck toward an *abnormal ground condition* is in such a condition. In order to apply this Rule, it must be known or virtually certain that the ball is in the *abnormal ground condition*. In the absence of such knowledge or certainty, the player must proceed under Rule 27-1.

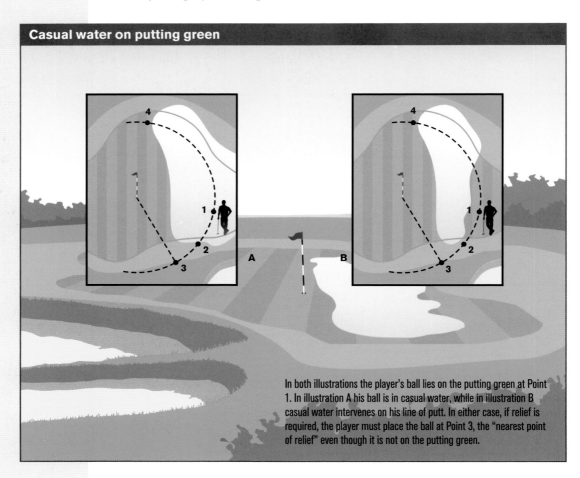

Casual water on putting green

In both illustrations the player's ball lies on the putting green at Point 1. In illustration A his ball is in casual water, while in illustration B casual water intervenes on his line of putt. In either case, if relief is required, the player must place the ball at Point 3, the "nearest point of relief" even though it is not on the putting green.

Ball close to casual water: left-handed stroke not reasonable

Ball close to casual water: left-handed stroke reasonable

Ball in casual water in bunker

I am taking relief from this casual water. Must I drop the ball at the nearest point of relief or may I drop it within one club-length of the nearest point of relief not nearer the hole?

As you are able to take complete relief from the casual water, you are allowed to drop within one club-length of the nearest point of relief. However, if complete relief had been impossible and you were taking maximum available relief, the ball would have to be dropped on the spot that gave maximum available relief.

If it is known or virtually certain that a ball that has not been found is in an *abnormal ground condition*, the player may take relief under this Rule. If he elects to do so, the spot where the ball last crossed the outermost limits of the *abnormal ground condition* must be determined and, for the purpose of applying this Rule, the ball is deemed to lie at this spot and the player must proceed as follows:

(i) Through the Green: If the ball last crossed the outermost limits of the *abnormal ground condition* at a spot *through the green*, the player may *substitute* another ball, without penalty, and take relief as prescribed in Rule 25-1b(i).

(ii) In a Bunker: If the ball last crossed the outermost limits of the *abnormal ground condition* at a spot in a *bunker*, the player may *substitute* another ball, without penalty, and take relief as prescribed in Rule 25-1b(ii).

(iii) In a Water Hazard (including a Lateral Water Hazard): If the ball last crossed the outermost limits of the *abnormal ground condition* at a spot in a *water hazard*, the player is not entitled to relief without penalty. The player must proceed under Rule 26-1.

(iv) On the Putting Green: If the ball last crossed the outermost limits of the *abnormal ground condition* at a spot on the *putting green*, the player may *substitute* another ball, without penalty, and take relief as prescribed in Rule 25-1b(iii).

Stance interfered with by burrowing animal hole: ball unplayable because of other condition

My ball is clearly unplayable in the roots of this tree. Can I take free relief because I would have to stand on a rabbit scrape if I was able to play it?

No. I am afraid you are not entitled to take a free drop because it is clearly unreasonable for you to play a stroke at your ball.

Embedded ball

My ball is plugged in the ground on the face of this bunker. What should I do?

Because the face is grass-covered it is not part of the bunker. It is not "closely mown" so you will have to play it as it lies or declare it unplayable. But at least you won't have to drop it in the bunker.

25-2 Embedded Ball

A ball embedded in its own pitch-mark in the ground in any closely-mown area *through the green* may be lifted, cleaned and dropped, without penalty, as near as possible to the spot where it lay but not nearer the *hole*. The ball when dropped must first strike a part of the *course through the green*. "Closely-mown area" means any area of the *course*, including paths through the rough, cut to fairway height or less.

25-3 Wrong Putting Green

25-3 a Interference

Interference by a *wrong putting green* occurs when a ball is on the *wrong putting green*.

Interference to a player's *stance* or the area of his intended swing is not, of itself, interference under this Rule.

25-3 b Relief

If a player's ball lies on a *wrong putting green*, he must not play the ball as it lies. He must take relief, without penalty, as follows:

The player must lift the ball and drop it within one club-length of and not nearer the *hole* than the *nearest point of relief*. The *nearest point of relief* must not be in a *hazard* or on a *putting green*. When dropping the ball within one club-length of the *nearest point of relief*, the ball must first strike a part of the *course* at a spot that avoids interference by the *wrong putting green* and is not in a *hazard* and not on a *putting green*. The ball may be cleaned when lifted under this Rule.

Penalty | For breach of Rule:
Match play – Loss of hole; **Stroke play** – Two strokes.

Relief from a wrong putting green

RULE 25

INCIDENTS

While playing in the penultimate group on the third day of the 2004 Masters Tournament, Ernie Els pulled his tee-shot into the trees at the par 4 11th hole. Although the South African managed to find his ball, it was lying badly in among some large, detached tree branches. It looked as if the player's only option would be to deem his ball unplayable, but Els asked Rules officials on the hole whether the branches may have been piled for removal, in which case they would constitute ground under repair (see Definition of "ground under repair") and he may be entitled to free relief. On first look, the officials did not feel that the branches had been piled for removal, but rather had been abandoned, in which case no free relief would be available. However, the officials agreed to get a second opinion from the Chairman of the Masters Rules Committee.

When the Chairman arrived on the scene he advised the player that the branches had come down in a recent ice storm and had been piled for removal. Els was shown where his nearest point of relief from the branches was and he dropped within one club-length of that point.

A very difficult shot back to the fairway through the trees still faced Els, but he played a great recovery shot and salvaged a bogey. This lucky break allowed Els to maintain his challenge to Phil Mickelson, with the American prevailing by one stroke over Els on the Sunday, after an historic tussle.

When his tee-shot dropped into some branches broken by a recent storm at Augusta National, Ernie Els was allowed free relief.

RULE 26 WATER HAZARDS (INCLUDING LATERAL WATER HAZARDS)

Definitions All defined terms are in *italics* and are listed alphabetically in the Definitions section – see pages 13–24.

26-1 Relief for Ball in Water Hazard

It is a question of fact whether a ball that has not been found after having been struck toward a *water hazard* is in the *hazard*. In order to apply this Rule, it must be known or virtually certain that the ball is in the *hazard*. In the absence of such knowledge or certainty, the player must proceed under Rule 27-1.

If a ball is in a *water hazard* or if it is known or virtually certain that a ball that has not been found is in a *water hazard* (whether the ball lies in water or not), the player may **under penalty of one stroke**:

a. Play a ball as nearly as possible at the spot from which the original ball was last played (see Rule 20-5); or

b. Drop a ball behind the *water hazard*, keeping the point at which the original ball last crossed the margin of the *water hazard* directly between the *hole* and the spot on which the ball is dropped, with no limit to how far behind the *water hazard* the ball may be dropped; or

c. As additional options available only if the ball last crossed the margin of a *lateral water hazard*, drop a ball outside the *water hazard* within two club-lengths of and not nearer the *hole* than (i) the point where the original ball last crossed the margin of the *water hazard* or (ii) a point on the opposite margin of the *water hazard* equidistant from the hole.

Jean Van de Velde's difficulty with the Barry Burn at the 72nd hole of the 1999 Open Championship at Carnoustie resulted in a three-way play-off for the Championship. See the details of his unfortunate brush with Rule 26-1 in the incident on pages 138–139.

When proceeding under this Rule, the player may lift and clean his ball or *substitute* a ball.

(Prohibited actions when ball is in a hazard – see Rule 13-4)

(Ball moving in water in a water hazard – see Rule 14-6)

26-2 Ball Played within Water Hazard

26-2 a Ball Comes to Rest in Same or Another Water Hazard

If a ball played from within a *water hazard* comes to rest in the same or another *water hazard* after the *stroke*, the player may:

(i) proceed under Rule 26-1a. If, after dropping in the *hazard*, the player elects not to play the dropped ball, he may:

(a) proceed under Rule 26-1b, or if applicable Rule 26-1c, adding the **additional penalty of one stroke** prescribed by the Rule and using as the reference point the point where the original ball last crossed the margin of this *hazard* before it came to rest in this *hazard*;

(b) add an additional penalty of one stroke and play a ball as nearly as possible at the spot from which the last *stroke* from outside a *water hazard* was made (see Rule 20-5); or

(ii) proceed under Rule 26-1b, or if applicable Rule 26-1c; or

(iii) under penalty of one stroke, play a ball as nearly as possible at the spot from which the last *stroke* from outside a *water hazard* was made (see Rule 20-5).

Ball crossing margin of water hazard

My ball crossed the water hazard, but spun back into it. Where do I take relief?

Under penalty of one stroke, you may play a ball from where you last played, or you may drop a ball behind the hazard on an extension of the line from the hole to the point at which the ball last crossed the margin (Point B). The point at which the ball first crossed the margin (Point A) is irrelevant.

26-2 b **Ball Lost or Unplayable Outside Hazard or Out of Bounds**

If a ball played from within a *water hazard* is *lost* or deemed unplayable outside the *hazard* or is *out of bounds*, the player may, after taking a **penalty of one stroke** under Rule 27-1 or 28a:

(i) play a ball as nearly as possible at the spot in the *hazard* from which the original ball was last played (see Rule 20-5); or

(ii) proceed under Rule 26-1b, or if applicable Rule 26-1c, **adding the additional penalty of one stroke** prescribed by the Rule and using as the reference point the point where the original ball last crossed the margin of the *hazard* before it came to rest in the *hazard*; or

(iii) **add an additional penalty of one stroke** and play a ball as nearly as possible at the spot from which the last *stroke* from outside a *water hazard* was made (see Rule 20-5).

Relief from lateral water hazard

The player has played a ball from the tee (Point A) into the lateral water hazard at Point B. It last crossed the margin of the hazard at Point C and the point on the opposite margin, equidistant from the hole is Point E. He may play the ball as it lies or, under penalty of one stroke; (i) play another ball from the tee – Rule 26-1a; (ii) drop a ball anywhere on the far side of the hazard on the dotted line from the hole through Point C, e.g. Point D – Rule 26-1b; (iii) drop a ball in the area on the near side of the hazard, which is all ground within two club-lengths of Point C – Rule 26-1c(i); or (iv) drop a ball in the area on the far side of the hazard, which is all ground within two club-lengths of Point E – Rule 26-1c(ii).

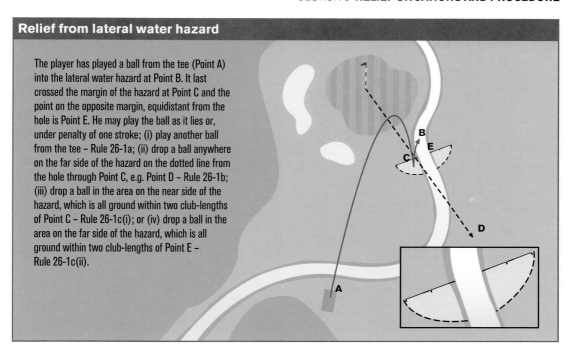

Ball played from within water hazard

The player's tee-shot at a par-3 hole comes to rest in a water hazard. He plays from the hazard, but fails to get his ball out. He may play the ball as it lies or, under penalty of one stroke: (i) drop a ball at the spot from which he's just played his second stroke and play again from there; (ii) drop a ball behind the hazard, anywhere on the dotted line, and play from there; or (iii) play another ball from the tee.

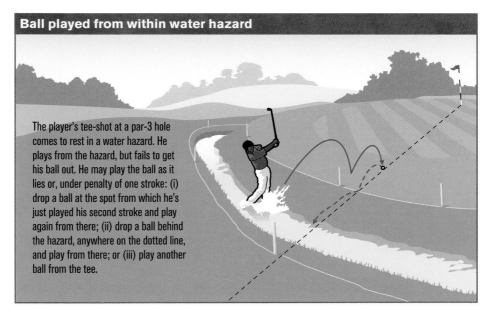

Note 1 When proceeding under Rule 26-2b, the player is not required to drop a ball under Rule 27-1 or 28a. If he does drop a ball, he is not required to play it. He may alternatively proceed under Rule 26-2b (ii) or (iii).

Note 2 If a ball played from within a *water hazard* is deemed unplayable outside the *hazard*, nothing in Rule 26-2b precludes the player from proceeding under Rule 28b or c.

Penalty **For breach of Rule:**
Match play – Loss of hole; **Stroke play** – Two strokes.

Oliver Fisher plays his ball, which had stopped short of the water hazard. Stakes and lines used to define the margin of or identify a lateral water hazard must be red.

RULE 26
INCIDENTS

Standing on Carnoustie's 18th tee, in the final round of the 1999 Open Championship, Jean Van de Velde needed only a double bogey to become the first Frenchman to win the Championship since 1907.

Minutes later, with his navy blue trousers rolled to his knees, he was standing in the Barry Burn contemplating his fate and his options under Rule 26.

Having played a driver from the tee, the Frenchman's ball had finished well right but safely on a peninsula created by a bend in the burn. Instead of laying up with his second, Van de Velde attempted to play a 2-iron to the distant green. His shot was a bit wayward and it ricocheted off a grandstand railing, the wall of the water hazard and finally settled behind the second crossing of the burn in heavy rough.

Attempting to hit his ball out of the rough and over the burn, he played it badly and the ball finished in the shallow water of the burn. As the stream runs perpendicular to the line of play, it was marked with a yellow line indicating a water hazard.

As such, Van de Velde had three options. He could play the ball without penalty as it lay. Additionally, under penalty of one stroke, he could play again from where he last played, or he could drop behind the hazard keeping the point at which his ball last crossed the margin of the water hazard directly between the hole and the spot on which the ball would be dropped, with no limit to how far behind the hazard he might want to go.

Three in the water, and needing a six to win The Open, the Frenchman contemplated playing out of the hazard in order to avoid the penalty stroke. To make such an assessment, he decided to go into the water to see what the shot required. Having removed his shoes and socks, Van de Velde rolled up his trouser legs and lowered himself down the stone wall into the shallow water.

Van de Velde was left standing alone in the dark water, wedge in hand, assessing his ability to play the submerged ball out of the hazard. After several minutes, discretion became the better part of valour and Van de Velde chose option b under Rule 26-1. He dropped a ball behind the hazard on the stipulated line, suffered a penalty stroke and played his fifth shot to the right greenside bunker. His up-and-down from the bunker resulted in a score of seven and a play-off between himself, Paul Lawrie and Justin Leonard, which Lawrie went on to win.

Tiger Woods went on to win the 2005 Masters despite putting into Rae's Creek at the 13th hole during his first round.

What was interesting about Tiger's incident was that it was obvious that he knew immediately that he had the option (under Rule 26-1a) of playing again from the spot from which he had initially putted, under penalty of one stroke. While it must have been daunting to face the same lightening-fast putt, his other option, which would have seen him drop on the fairway side of the water hazard (keeping the point where the ball crossed the hazard margin and the flagstick in a direct line), was clearly less desirable.

Another point to note about Tiger's chosen procedure was that, as the next stroke was being made from where the previous stroke had been played, in accordance with Rule 20-5, Woods was required to place a ball on the putting green, rather than drop it. He also chose not to retrieve the original ball from the water and, instead, substituted another ball, which the player is always entitled to do under Rule 26.

FAQ

Q What differentiates a water hazard from a lateral water hazard?
A A water hazard is any sea, lake, pond, river, ditch, surface drainage ditch or other open water course (whether or not containing water) and anything of a similar nature – see the Definition of "water hazard". If a player's ball lies in a water hazard, he may play the ball as it lies or proceed under Rule 26-1a or b.

A lateral water hazard is a water hazard or that part of a water hazard so situated that it is not possible or is deemed by the Committee to be impracticable to drop a ball behind the water hazard in accordance with Rule 26-1b – see Definition of "lateral water hazard". If a player's ball lies in a lateral water hazard, he may, in addition to the options available when in a water hazard, proceed under Rule 26-1c. Stakes and lines defining a water hazard must be yellow. Stakes and lines defining a lateral water hazard must be red.

RULE 27
BALL LOST OR OUT OF BOUNDS; PROVISIONAL BALL

Definitions   All defined terms are in *italics* and are listed alphabetically in the Definitions section – see pages 13–24.

27-1   Stroke and Distance; Ball Out of Bounds; Ball Not Found Within Five Minutes

27-1 a   Proceeding Under Stroke and Distance

At any time, a player may, **under penalty of one stroke**, play a ball as nearly as possible at the spot from which the original ball was last played (see Rule 20-5) i.e., proceed under penalty of stroke and distance.

Except as otherwise provided in the *Rules*, if a player makes a *stroke* at a ball from the spot at which the original ball was last played, he is deemed to have proceeded under penalty of stroke and distance.

27-1 b   Ball Out of Bounds

If a ball is *out of bounds*, the player must play a ball, **under penalty of one stroke**, as nearly as possible at the spot from which the original ball was last played (see Rule 20-5).

27-1 c   Ball Not Found Within Five Minutes

If a ball is *lost* as a result of not being found or identified as his by the player within five minutes after the player's *side* or his or their *caddies* have begun to search for it, the player must play a ball, **under penalty of one stroke**, as nearly as possible at the spot from which the original ball was last played (see Rule 20-5).

Players unable to identify their balls

My ball is a number 3 with black writing.

So is mine. Unless we can identify which is which, both balls are "lost".

Ball found within five minutes

Thanks for finding my ball and calling me back before I played another ball. We hadn't been looking for it for five minutes, so I'll play it.

That's OK. Your ball wasn't "lost" merely because you went back to play another ball before the five minutes search was up. But if you had played another ball before I called you back that would have become the ball in play and this one would have been "lost". In that situation you couldn't have played on with it.

Exceptions

1 If it is known or virtually certain that the original ball that has not been found, is in an *obstruction* (Rule 24-3) or is in an *abnormal ground condition* (Rule 25-1c), the player may proceed under the applicable Rule.

2 If it is known or virtually certain that the original ball that has not been found has been moved by an *outside agency* (Rule 18-1) or is in a *water hazard*, (Rule 26-1), the player must proceed under the applicable Rule.

Penalty

For breach of Rule 27-1:
Match play – Loss of hole; **Stroke play** – Two strokes.

27-2 Provisional Ball

27-2 a Procedure

If a ball may be *lost* outside a *water hazard* or may be *out of bounds*, to save time the player may play another ball provisionally in accordance with Rule 27-1. The player must inform his opponent in match play or his *marker* or a *fellow-competitor* in stroke play that he intends to play a *provisional ball*, and he must play it before he or his *partner* goes forward to search for the original ball.

If he fails to do so and plays another ball, that ball is not a *provisional ball* and becomes the *ball in play* **under penalty of stroke and distance** (Rule 27-1); the original ball is *lost*.

(Order of play from teeing ground – see Rule 10-3)

Note

If a *provisional ball* played under Rule 27-2a might be *lost* outside a *water hazard* or *out of bounds*, the player may play another *provisional ball*. If another *provisional ball* is played, it bears the same relationship to the previous *provisional ball* as the first *provisional ball* bears to the original ball.

27-2 b | **When Provisional Ball Becomes Ball in Play**

The player may play a *provisional ball* until he reaches the place where the original ball is likely to be. If he makes a *stroke* with the *provisional ball* from the place where the original ball is likely to be or from a point nearer the *hole* than that place, the original ball is *lost* and the *provisional ball* becomes the *ball in play* **under penalty of stroke and distance** (Rule 27-1).

If the original ball is *lost* outside a *water hazard* or is *out of bounds*, the *provisional ball* becomes the *ball in play*, **under penalty of stroke and distance** (Rule 27-1).

If it is known or virtually certain that the original ball is in a *water hazard*, the player must proceed in accordance with Rule 26-1.

Exception | If it is known or virtually certain that the original ball is in an *obstruction* (Rule 24-3) or an *abnormal ground condition* (Rule 25-1c), the player may proceed under the applicable Rule.

27-2 c | **When Provisional Ball to be Abandoned**

If the original ball is neither *lost* nor *out of bounds*, the player must abandon the *provisional ball* and continue play with the original ball. If he makes any further *strokes* at the *provisional ball*, he is playing a *wrong ball* and the provisions of Rule 15-3 apply.

Note | If a player plays a *provisional ball* under Rule 27-2a, the *strokes* made after this Rule has been invoked with a *provisional ball* subsequently abandoned under Rule 27-2c and *penalty strokes* incurred solely by playing that ball are disregarded.

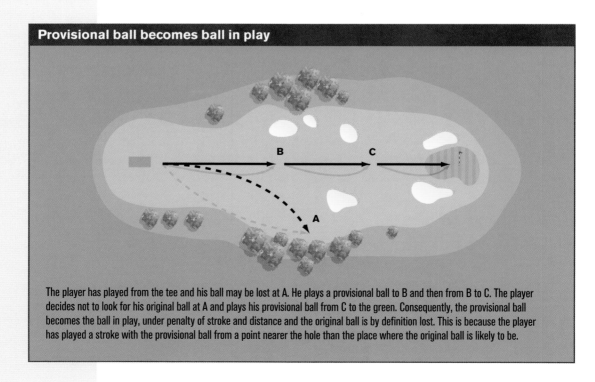

Provisional ball becomes ball in play

The player has played from the tee and his ball may be lost at A. He plays a provisional ball to B and then from B to C. The player decides not to look for his original ball at A and plays his provisional ball from C to the green. Consequently, the provisional ball becomes the ball in play, under penalty of stroke and distance and the original ball is by definition lost. This is because the player has played a stroke with the provisional ball from a point nearer the hole than the place where the original ball is likely to be.

Provisional ball played: original ball found unplayable

A player plays a provisional ball as his ball may be lost. The original ball is found within five minutes and before the provisional ball has become the ball in play, but the ball is unplayable. The player must abandon the provisional ball and proceed with the original.

RULE **27**

INCIDENTS

During the third round of the 1998 Open Championship at Royal Birkdale, Mark O'Meara's second shot drifted too far to the right into knee-high grass and gorse at the 480-yard 6th hole and put into motion a series of events that led to the introduction of a clarifying Decision.

By the time O'Meara and his caddie reached the area where they thought his ball had landed, a number of spectators were already engaged in searching for it. The Rules observer with the group started the clock for the five-minute search period when O'Meara and his caddie arrived.

Several balls were found, but none were O'Meara's. To everyone in the immediate vicinity, he announced the type of ball he was using and stated that it was embossed with his logo.

After searching for approximately four minutes, O'Meara suspected that his ball was lost. He left the search area, took another ball from his caddie and started back down the fairway to play again from where his original ball had been played.

About 30 seconds later, a spectator announced, "Here it is. I have it." Someone called to O'Meara, who apparently did not hear and continued walking. An official went to where the spectator had found the ball and saw it was the type O'Meara was using and did have his logo on it.

By this time, it was nearing the end of the five-minute search period permitted under the Rules and it was clear that O'Meara would not be able to get back to the ball in order to identify it within the five-minute period. The Definition of "Lost Ball" states that a ball is lost if it is not "found or identified" within five minutes. If the definition said "found and identified", the procedure would have been clear. A radio call was made for a roving Rules official to make a decision.

The roving official arrived on the scene and brought O'Meara in a cart back up the fairway where a discussion took place. A further official arrived and it was determined that the ball had been found within the five-minute period, that

Mark O'Meara returns to identify a ball found within the five-minute search period during the 1998 Open Championship.

O'Meara was entitled to identify it outside the stipulated time period and, if it was his ball, he was entitled to play it, so everyone returned to the area where the ball had been found.

However, during the search, the search area had been trampled and a misguided spectator, who believed the ball had been abandoned, had lifted it. When O'Meara and the official went to the spot, the ball was not there but the spectator was close by and returned the ball to O'Meara who identified it as his. Although the spectator said he knew "exactly" where the ball had been before he lifted it, that turned out to be only an approximation.

Under Rules 18-1 and 20-3c, O'Meara was required to drop as nearly as possible to the spot where the ball had been before being lifted by the spectator. When O'Meara dropped the ball, it rolled more than two club-lengths from the spot where it struck a part of the course thus requiring a re-drop. Upon re-dropping, the ball rolled nearer to the hole and O'Meara, therefore, placed it on the spot where it first struck a part of the course when re-dropped. He then played his shot and continued the round, winning the Championship the following day.

The ambiguity of the Definition of "Lost Ball", in this particular situation, necessitated the addition of Decision 27/5.5. That decision clarifies that if a ball is found within five minutes, the player is allowed enough time to reach the area and identify it even though the identification takes place after the five-minute search period has elapsed.

Another golfer to make a remarkable par recovery from a lost-ball situation was Gary Evans. Having played his way into contention by achieving seven under on the first 16 holes of the final day of the 2002 Open Championship at Muirfield,

Evans hooked his second shot at the par-5 17th into deep rough on the outside of the spectator ropes, which sparked a frantic, and ultimately unsuccessful, search.

The clock starts when the player or his caddie has begun to search for a ball, so when spectators started searching for Evans' ball before the player arrived in the area this initial search did not form part of the five-minute period. A player cannot keep away from the area and then claim that, as he has not begun to search, the clock has not started. In such circumstances, a Rules official would have to begin timing when he felt that the player had been given reasonable opportunity to reach the area and begin his search. However, Evans and his caddie got to the area in good time and joined the mass of spectators looking for the ball. Evans could be heard pleading with the crowd to look at the ground rather than looking at him.

Remarkably, with more than 50 people hunting for the ball, it was not to be found. The Rules official walking with the game advised Evans that the five-minute period had elapsed, and Evans had to take the long walk back to where he had played his second shot and put another ball into play under penalty of stroke and distance (Rule 27-1).

At The Open there is a condition of competition that prohibits the use of transport unless authorised by the Committee. If there is a roving Rules official on hand with a cart, a player returning to put another ball into play will be offered a ride by the Rules official, who can authorise this as a member of the Committee. Evans was given this opportunity, but chose to walk back, perhaps in order to gather his thoughts before playing his fourth stroke. This seemed to work, because Evans hit a great shot on to the 17th green and followed that with an amazing putt to save par.

Two balls were found when Gary Evans drove into the rough on the 17th hole at Muirfield, but neither of them belonged to him. One in fact was a Titleist 2, which was the same type of ball that Evans was using, but it did not have his identification mark on it. This highlighted the importance of putting an identification mark on the ball in order to avoid wrong-ball penalties.

BALL UNPLAYABLE

Definitions

All defined terms are in *italics* and are listed alphabetically in the Definitions section – see pages 13–24.

The player may deem his ball unplayable at any place on the *course* except when the ball is in a *water hazard*. The player is the sole judge as to whether his ball is unplayable.

If the player deems his ball to be unplayable, he must **under penalty of one stroke**:

a. Play a ball as nearly as possible at the spot from which the original ball was last played (see Rule 20-5); or

b. Drop a ball behind the point where the ball lay, keeping that point directly between the *hole* and the spot on which the ball is dropped, with no limit to how far behind that point the ball may be dropped; or

c. Drop a ball within two club-lengths of the spot where the ball lay, but not nearer the *hole*; or

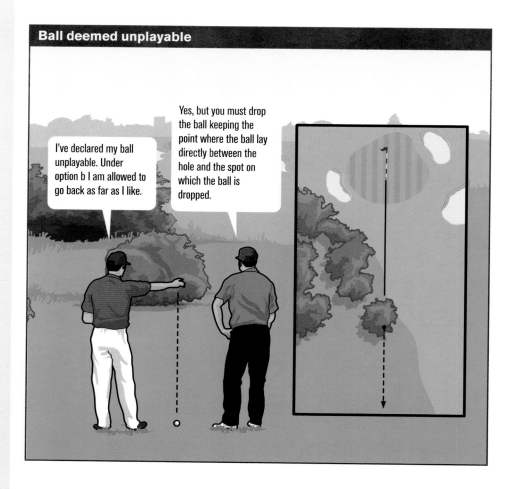

Ball deemed unplayable

I've declared my ball unplayable. Under option b I am allowed to go back as far as I like.

Yes, but you must drop the ball keeping the point where the ball lay directly between the hole and the spot on which the ball is dropped.

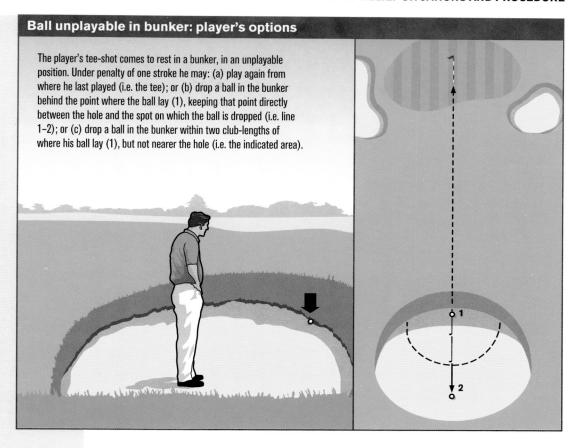

Ball unplayable in bunker: player's options

The player's tee-shot comes to rest in a bunker, in an unplayable position. Under penalty of one stroke he may: (a) play again from where he last played (i.e. the tee); or (b) drop a ball in the bunker behind the point where the ball lay (1), keeping that point directly between the hole and the spot on which the ball is dropped (i.e. line 1–2); or (c) drop a ball in the bunker within two club-lengths of where his ball lay (1), but not nearer the hole (i.e. the indicated area).

If the unplayable ball is in a *bunker*, the player may proceed under Clause a, b, or c. If he elects to proceed under Clause b or c, a ball must be dropped in the *bunker*.

When proceeding under this Rule, the player may lift and clean his ball or *substitute* a ball.

Penalty

For breach of Rule:
Match play – Loss of hole; **Stroke play** – Two strokes.

RULE 28

INCIDENTS

Former Ryder Cup player Pierre Fulke had an unusual incident at Wentworth's 16th hole during the 2004 PGA Championship. Fulke pulled his tee-shot into the trees on the left of the hole and found his ball in an unplayable lie. The option under Rule 28b of dropping back on a line with the flagstick did not provide Fulke with any relief, so he examined the option of dropping within two club-lengths of where the ball lay (Rule 28c). He found that the only place within two club-lengths where he could obtain a playable lie was within a dry lateral water hazard. The player also thought that, if he dropped the ball in the dry ditch and it transpired that he could not play the dropped ball, he would then have the option of dropping out of the hazard under a further penalty of one stroke under Rule 26-1c.

At this point, a Rules official arrived on the scene and was quick to advise Fulke that if he did drop the ball in the lateral water hazard and could not play it, his only option would be to proceed under the stroke and distance element of the water hazard Rule (Rule 26-1a). This is due to the fact that the player would not have a reference point where the ball last crossed the margin of the hazard, as the ball would have been dropped in the hazard rather than entering it as a result of a stroke. The authority for the official's advice is found in Decision 28/4.5, which, remarkably, was introduced in 1998 following an identical incident involving Eamonn Darcy at the very same hole.

Fulke decided that the possibility of incurring two penalty strokes (one under the unplayable ball Rule and one under the water hazard Rule), and then potentially having to return to the tee, was too much of a risk. Consequently, he opted to proceed directly under the stroke and distance option of the unplayable ball Rule (Rule 28a) and returned to the tee, where he played his third shot.

FAQ

Q Must the position of a ball be marked when taking a drop from an immovable obstruction, an abnormal ground condition or because the ball is considered to be unplayable (i.e. under Rules 24, 25 or 28)?

A The position of a ball need only be marked when it is lifted under a Rule that requires it to be replaced: for example, Rule 16-1b or 20-1. A ball to be dropped or placed in any other position, such as when taking relief from an immovable obstruction, an abnormal ground condition or an unplayable lie, does not need to be marked. However, a player is strongly advised to do so, as it is considered good practice.

RULE 29 THREESOMES AND FOURSOMES

Definitions All defined terms are in *italics* and are listed alphabetically in the Definitions section – see pages 13–24.

29-1 General

In a *threesome* or a *foursome*, during any *stipulated round* the *partners* must play alternately from the *teeing grounds* and alternately during the play of each hole. *Penalty strokes* do not affect the order of play.

29-2 Match Play

If a player plays when his *partner* should have played, **his side loses the hole**.

29-3 Stroke Play

If the *partners* make a *stroke* or *strokes* in incorrect order, such *stroke* or *strokes* are cancelled and **the side incurs a penalty of two strokes**. The *side* must correct the error by playing a ball in correct order as nearly as possible at the spot from which it first played in incorrect order (see Rule 20-5). If the *side* makes a *stroke* on the next *teeing ground* without first correcting the error or, in the case of the last hole of the round, leaves the *putting green* without declaring its intention to correct the error, **the side is disqualified**.

Foursomes: order of play when partner drives out-of-bounds

That's miles out-of-bounds. What happens now in a mixed foursome?

Your partner must play your side's third shot from the men's tee because that's where the last shot was played from.

Foursomes: which partner drops the ball

See Rule 20-2a, which requires a ball to be dropped by the player himself.

Order of play in 36-hole competition

Rule 29-1. See Definition of "stipulated round".

RULE 29

INCIDENTS

The practice putting green at the Old Course in St Andrews lies just off the course and only a few steps from the 1st tee. Paired together on the second day for the morning foursomes of the 1975 Walker Cup Match, the US side of veteran William C. Campbell and newcomer John Grace reported to the tee a little ahead of time. They had already decided that Grace would drive at the odd-numbered holes, so Campbell decided to use the extra time before the match began to walk to the practice green and hit a few putts.

As the visiting team, Campbell and Grace had the honour. The wind was blowing from the west off St Andrews Bay, which carried the announcement of the match's beginning beyond Campbell's earshot.

As the breeze momentarily died, Campbell heard "the click" of Grace's drive just before striking a practice putt, and he was unable to interrupt his stroke. He had practised during the play of the hole. Instantly and instinctively recognising his breach, Campbell walked on to the fairway and reported to the referee that the US had lost the first hole (Rule 7-2 and Rule 29).

The Referee for the match accepted Campbell's report but made no immediate announcement to the other players. Because play of the hole had ended with the breach of Rule 7-2, Campbell was free to play his side's second from where Grace's good drive lay to the green, as simply more practice.

Walking across the Swilcan Burn, Campbell told Grace what had taken place. "He was incredulous, to say the least," Campbell recalls.

The Americans lost the first hole and eventually lost the match to Mark James and Richard Eyles.

RULE 30

THREE-BALL, BEST-BALL AND FOUR-BALL MATCH PLAY

Definitions

All defined terms are in *italics* and are listed alphabetically in the Definitions section – see pages 13–24.

30-1

Rules of Golf Apply
The Rules of Golf, so far as they are not at variance with the following specific Rules, apply to *three-ball*, *best-ball* and *four-ball matches*.

30-2

Three-Ball Match Play

30-2 a

Ball at Rest Moved by an Opponent
Except as otherwise provided in the *Rules*, if the player's ball is touched or *moved* by an opponent, his *caddie* or *equipment* other than during search, Rule 18-3b applies. **That opponent incurs a penalty of one stroke in his match with the player,** but not in his match with the other opponent.

30-2 b   **Ball Deflected or Stopped by an Opponent Accidentally**

If a player's ball is accidentally deflected or stopped by an opponent, his *caddie* or *equipment*, there is no penalty. In his match with that opponent the player may, before another *stroke* is made by either *side*, cancel the *stroke* and play a ball, without penalty, as nearly as possible at the spot from which the original ball was last played (see Rule 20-5) or he may play the ball as it lies. In his match with the other opponent, the ball must be played as it lies.

Exception   Ball striking person attending or holding up *flagstick* or anything carried by him – see Rule 17-3b.

(Ball purposely deflected or stopped by opponent – see Rule 1-2)

30-3   Best-Ball and Four-Ball Match Play

30-3 a   **Representation of Side**

A *side* may be represented by one *partner* for all or any part of a match; all *partners* need not be present. An absent *partner* may join a match between holes, but not during play of a hole.

30-3b   **Order of Play**

Balls belonging to the same *side* may be played in the order the *side* considers best.

Breach of rule by one partner in match play

I'll just remove this twig.

I'm afraid you're disqualified from the hole for removing a loose impediment from the bunker. Fortunately, although I'm in the same bunker I'm not penalised because your breach of Rule 13-4 did not assist my play.

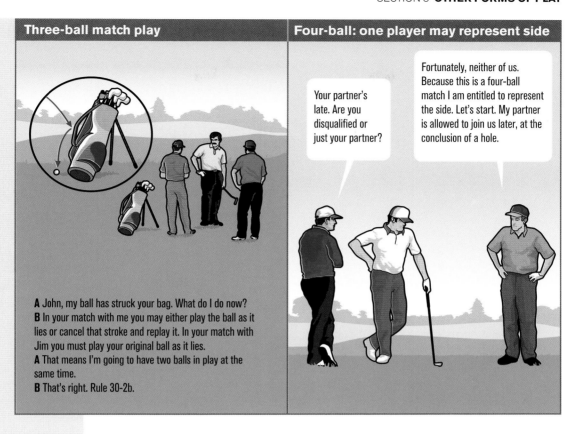

Three-ball match play

A John, my ball has struck your bag. What do I do now?
B In your match with me you may either play the ball as it lies or cancel that stroke and replay it. In your match with Jim you must play your original ball as it lies.
A That means I'm going to have two balls in play at the same time.
B That's right. Rule 30-2b.

Four-ball: one player may represent side

Your partner's late. Are you disqualified or just your partner?

Fortunately, neither of us. Because this is a four-ball match I am entitled to represent the side. Let's start. My partner is allowed to join us later, at the conclusion of a hole.

30-3 c | **Wrong Ball**

If a player incurs the loss of hole penalty under Rule 15-3a for making a *stroke* at a *wrong ball*, **he is disqualified for that hole**, but his *partner* incurs no penalty even if the *wrong ball* belongs to him. If the *wrong ball* belongs to another player, its owner must place a ball on the spot from which the *wrong ball* was first played.

30-3 d | **Penalty to Side**

A *side* is penalised for a breach of any of the following by any *partner*:
• Rule 4   Clubs
• Rule 6-4   Caddie
• Any Local Rule or Condition of Competition for which the penalty is an adjustment to the state of the match.

30-3 e | **Disqualification of Side**

(i) **A *side* is disqualified** if any *partner* incurs a penalty for disqualification under any of the following:
• Rule 1-3   Agreement to Waive Rules
• Rule 4   Clubs
• Rule 5-1 or 5-2 The Ball
• Rule 6-2a   Handicap
• Rule 6-4   Caddie

- Rule 6-7   Undue Delay; Slow Play
- Rule 11-1   Teeing
- Rule 14-3   Artificial Devices, Unusual Equipment and Unusual Use of Equipment
- Rule 33-7   Disqualification Penalty Imposed by Committee

(ii) A *side* is **disqualified** if all *partners* incur a penalty of disqualification under any of the following:

- Rule 6-3   Time of Starting and Groups
- Rule 6-8   Discontinuance of Play

(iii) In all other cases where a breach of a *Rule* would result in disqualification, **the player is disqualified for that hole only.**

30-3 f   **Effect of Other Penalties**

If a player's breach of a *Rule* assists his *partner's* play or adversely affects an opponent's play, **the *partner* incurs the applicable penalty in addition to any penalty incurred by the player.**

Here Jim Furyk confers with his playing partner Tiger Woods at the 2006 Ryder Cup. Under Rule 30-3b, in match play it is up to each side to decide in which order their balls are played (see incident on page 155).

In all other cases where a player incurs a penalty for breach of a *Rule*, the penalty does not apply to his *partner*. Where the penalty is stated to be loss of hole, the effect is to disqualify the player for that hole.

RULE 30
INCIDENTS

During one of the 2006 Ryder Cup four-ball matches, the American duo Tiger Woods and Jim Furyk were up against Darren Clarke and Lee Westwood, for the European team. While playing the 7th hole at The K Club, Woods hit his second shot into the water behind the green and was not planning to continue the play of the hole, as permitted in match play. Of the remaining three balls, Clarke was farthest away from the hole but Jim Furyk wanted to play first. Although Woods was not going to complete the hole, his ball lying in the water was obviously the farthest away from the hole and, as Rule 30-3b provides that a side may play in the order it considers best, it was Tiger's "honour" and, therefore, Furyk was entitled to play first.

The American duo raised the question of whether Woods had to drop a ball first as he clearly could not play the one in the water. However, the Rules official with the match confirmed that the relevant point for determining the order of play is the spot where the ball lies in the water hazard, not where it might be dropped, so dropping was not necessary (see the Note to Rule 10-1b).

RULE 31
FOUR-BALL STROKE PLAY

Definitions
All defined terms are in *italics* and are listed alphabetically in the Definitions section – see pages 13–24.

31-1 General
The Rules of Golf, so far as they are not at variance with the following specific Rules, apply to *four-ball* stroke play.

31-2 Representation of Side
A *side* may be represented by either *partner* for all or any part of a *stipulated round*; both *partners* need not be present. An absent *competitor* may join his *partner* between holes, but not during play of a hole.

31-3 Scoring
The *marker* is required to record for each hole only the gross score of whichever *partner's* score is to count. The gross scores to count must be individually identifiable; otherwise **the *side* is disqualified**. Only one of the *partners* need be responsible for complying with Rule 6-6b.
(Wrong score – see Rule 31-7a)

Four-ball stroke play

Date _3RD APRIL 2006_

Competition _SPRING OPEN FOUR-BALL_

PLAYER A _J. SUTHERLAND_ Handicap _16_ Strokes _12_

PLAYER B _W.B. TAYLOR_ Handicap _12_ Strokes _9_

Hole	Length Yards	Par	Stroke Index	Gross Score A	Gross Score B	Net Score A	Net Score B	Won X Lost – Half O	Mar. Score	Hole	Length Yards	Par	Stroke Index	Gross Score A	Gross Score B	Net Score A	Net Score B	Won X Lost – Half O	Mar. Score
1	437	4	4			4	3			10	425	4	3		5		4		
2	320	4	14			4	4			11	141	3	17	3		3			
3	162	3	18			4	4			12	476	5	9	6		5			
4	504	5	7	6		5				13	211	3	11			4	4		
5	181	3	16	4		4				14	437	4	5			5	4		
6	443	4	2		5	4				15	460	4	1			5	4		
7	390	4	8		5	4				16	176	3	15	4		4			
8	346	4	12	5		4				17	340	4	13	4		4			
9	340	4	10	4		3				18	435	4	6	6		5			
Out	3123	35				35				In	3101	34				37			
										Out	3123	35				35			
										T'tl	6224	69				72			
										Handicap									
										Net Score									

Player's Signature _J. Sutherland_

Marker's Signature _R.J. Parker_

Partner's scores to be individually identified

1 The lower score of the partners is the score for the hole (Rule 31).

2 Only one of the partners need be responsible for complying with Rule 6-6b, i.e. recording scores, checking scores, countersigning and returning the card (Rule 31-3).

3 The competitor is solely responsible for the correctness of the gross score recorded. Although there is no objection to the competitor (or his marker) entering the net score, it is the Committee's responsibility to record the better ball score for each hole, to add up the scores and to apply the handicaps recorded on the card (Rule 33-5). Thus there is no penalty for an error by the competitor (or his marker) for recording an incorrect net score.

4 Scores of the two partners must be kept in separate columns otherwise it is impossible for the Committee to apply the correct handicap. If the scores of both partners, having different handicaps, are recorded in the same column, the Committee has no alternative but to disqualify both partners (Rules 31-7 and 6-6 apply).

5 The Committee is responsible for laying down the conditions under which a competition is to be played (Rule 33-1), including the method of handicapping. In the above illustration the Committee laid down that $\frac{3}{4}$ handicaps would apply.

31-4   Order of Play

Balls belonging to the same *side* may be played in the order the *side* considers best.

31-5   Wrong Ball

If a *competitor* is in breach of Rule 15-3b for making a *stroke* at a *wrong ball*, **he incurs a penalty of two strokes** and must correct his mistake by playing the correct ball or by proceeding under the *Rules*. His *partner* incurs no penalty even if the *wrong ball* belongs to him.

    If the *wrong ball* belongs to another *competitor*, its owner must place a ball on the spot from which the *wrong ball* was first played.

31-6   Penalty to Side

A *side* is penalised for a breach of any of the following by any *partner*:
• Rule 4   Clubs
• Rule 6-4   Caddie
• Any Local Rule or Condition of Competition for which there is a maximum penalty per round.

31-7   Disqualification Penalties

31-7 a   Breach by One Partner

A *side* is disqualified from the competition if either *partner* incurs a penalty of disqualification under any of the following:
• Rule 1-3   Agreement to Waive Rules
• Rule 3-4   Refusal to Comply with a Rule
• Rule 4   Clubs
• Rule 5-1 or 5-2 The Ball
• Rule 6-2b   Handicap
• Rule 6-4   Caddie
• Rule 6-6b   Signing and Returning Score Card
• Rule 6-6d   Wrong Score for Hole
• Rule 6-7   Undue Delay; Slow Play
• Rule 7-1   Practice Before or Between Rounds
• Rule 11-1   Teeing
• Rule 14-3   Artificial Devices, Unusual Equipment and Unusual Use of Equipment
• Rule 22-1   Ball Assisting Play
• Rule 31-3   Gross Scores to Count Not Individually Identifiable
• Rule 33-7   Disqualification Penalty Imposed by Committee

31-7 b   Breach by Both Partners

A *side* is disqualified from the competition:

(i) if each *partner* incurs a penalty of disqualification for a breach of Rule 6-3 (Time of Starting and Groups) or Rule 6-8 (Discontinuance of Play), or

(ii) if, at the same hole, each *partner* is in breach of a *Rule* the penalty for which is disqualification from the competition or for a hole.

31-7 c **For the Hole Only**

In all other cases where a breach of a *Rule* would result in disqualification, **the competitor is disqualified only for the hole at which the breach occurred.**

31-8 **Effect of Other Penalties**

If a *competitor's* breach of a *Rule* assists his *partner's* play, **the *partner* incurs the applicable penalty in addition to any penalty incurred by the *competitor*.**

In all other cases where a *competitor* incurs a penalty for breach of a *Rule*, the penalty does not apply to his *partner*.

RULE 32 BOGEY, PAR AND STABLEFORD COMPETITIONS

Definitions All defined terms are in *italics* and are listed alphabetically in the Definitions section – see pages 13–24.

32-1 **Conditions**

Bogey, par and Stableford competitions are forms of stroke play in which play is against a fixed score at each hole. The *Rules* for stroke play, so far as they are not at variance with the following specific Rules, apply.

In handicap bogey, par and Stableford competitions, the *competitor* with the lowest net score at a hole takes the *honour* at the next *teeing ground*.

32-1 a **Bogey and Par Competitions**

The scoring for bogey and par competitions is made as in match play. Any hole for which a *competitor* makes no return is regarded as a loss. The winner is the *competitor* who is most successful in the aggregate of holes.

The *marker* is responsible for marking only the gross number of *strokes* for each hole where the *competitor* makes a net score equal to or less than the fixed score.

Note 1 If a *competitor's* score is adjusted by **deducting a hole or holes** under the applicable *Rule* when a penalty other than disqualification is incurred under any of the following:
• Rule 4   Clubs
• Rule 6-4   Caddie
• Any Local Rule or Condition of Competition for which there is a maximum penalty per round.
The *competitor* is responsible for reporting the facts regarding such a breach to the *Committee* before he returns his score card so that the *Committee* may apply the penalty. If the *competitor* fails to report his breach to the *Committee*, **he is disqualified.**

Note 2 If the competitor is in breach of Rule 6-7 (Undue Delay; Slow Play), the *Committee* will **deduct one hole** from the aggregate of holes. For a repeated offence, see Rule 32-2a.

32-1 b   **Stableford Competitions**

The scoring in Stableford competitions is made by points awarded in relation to a fixed score at each hole as follows:

Hole Played In	Points
More than one over fixed score or no score returned	0
One over fixed score	1
Fixed score	2
One under fixed score	3
Two under fixed score	4
Three under fixed score	5
Four under fixed score	6

The winner is the *competitor* who scores the highest number of points.

The *marker* is responsible for marking only the gross number of *strokes* at each hole where the *competitor's* net score earns one or more points.

Note 1   If a *competitor* is in breach of a *Rule* for which there is a maximum penalty per round, he must report the facts to the *Committee* before returning his score card; if he fails to do so, **he is disqualified.** The *Committee* will, from the total points scored for the round, **deduct two points for each hole at which any breach occurred, with a maximum dedcution per round of four points for each *Rule* breached.**

Note 2   If the *competitor* is in breach of Rule 6-7 (Undue Delay; Slow Play), the *Committee* will **deduct two points from the total points scored for the round. For a repeat offence, see Rule 32-2a.**

32-2   **Disqualification Penalties**

32-2 a   **From the Competition**

A *competitor* is disqualified from the competition if he incurs a penalty of disqualification under any of the following:
- Rule 1-3   Agreement to Waive Rules
- Rule 3-4   Refusal to Comply with a Rule
- Rule 4   Clubs
- Rule 5-1 or 5-2 The Ball
- Rule 6-2b   Handicap
- Rule 6-3   Time of Starting and Groups
- Rule 6-4   Caddie
- Rule 6-6b   Signing and Returning Score Card
- Rule 6-6d   Wrong Score for Hole, i.e. when the recorded score is lower than actually taken, except that no penalty is incurred when a breach of this Rule does not affect the result of the hole
- Rule 6-7   Undue Delay; Slow Play
- Rule 6-8   Discontinuance of Play
- Rule 7-1   Practice Before or Between Rounds

- Rule 11-1   Teeing
- Rule 14-3   Artificial Devices, Unusual Equipment and Unusual Use
                     of Equipment
- Rule 22-1   Ball Assisting Play
- Rule 33-7   Disqualification Penalty Imposed by Committee

32-2 b   **For a Hole**

In all other cases where a breach of a *Rule* would result in disqualification, **the competitor is disqualified only for the hole at which the breach occurred.**

RULE 33

THE COMMITTEE

Definitions   All defined terms are in *italics* and are listed alphabetically in the Definitions section – see pages 13–24.

33-1   **Conditions; Waiving Rule**

The *Committee* must establish the conditions under which a competition is to be played.

The *Committee* has no power to waive a Rule of Golf.

Certain specific *Rules* governing stroke play are so substantially different from those governing match play that combining the two forms of play is not practicable and is not permitted. The result of a match played in these circumstances is null and void and, in the stroke play competition, the *competitors* are disqualified.

In stroke play the *Committee* may limit a *referee's* duties.

33-2   **The Course**

33-2 a   **Defining Bounds and Margins**

The *Committee* must define accurately:

(i) the *course* and *out of bounds*,

(ii) the margins of *water hazards* and *lateral water hazards*,

(iii) *ground under repair*, and

(iv) *obstructions* and integral parts of the *course*.

33-2 b   **New Holes**

New *holes* should be made on the day on which a stroke play competition begins and at such other times as the *Committee* considers necessary, provided all *competitors* in a single round play with each *hole* cut in the same position.

Exception   When it is impossible for a damaged *hole* to be repaired so that it conforms with the Definition, the *Committee* may make a new *hole* in a nearby similar position.

If the course is not in a playable condition, the Committee may have to temporarily suspend play. In stroke play only, if further play becomes impossible, the Committee may have to declare play null and void.

Note   Where a single round is to be played on more than one day, the *Committee* may provide, in the conditions of a competition (Rule 33-1), that the *holes* and *teeing grounds* may be differently situated on each day of the competition, provided that, on any one day, all *competitors* play with each *hole* and each *teeing ground* in the same position.

33-2 c   **Practice Ground**

Where there is no practice ground available outside the area of a competition *course*, the *Committee* should establish the area on which players may practise on any day of a competition, if it is practicable to do so. On any day of a stroke play competition, the *Committee* should not normally permit practice on or to a *putting green* or from a *hazard* of the competition *course*.

33-2 d | **Course Unplayable**

If the *Committee* or its authorised representative considers that for any reason the *course* is not in a playable condition or that there are circumstances that render the proper playing of the game impossible, it may, in match play or stroke play, order a temporary suspension of play or, in stroke play, declare play null and void and cancel all scores for the round in question. When a round is cancelled, all penalties incurred in that round are cancelled. (Procedure in discontinuing and resuming play – see Rule 6-8)

33-3 Times of Starting and Groups

The *Committee* must establish the times of starting and, in stroke play, arrange the groups in which *competitors* must play.

When a match play competition is played over an extended period, the *Committee* establishes the limit of time within which each round must be completed. When players are allowed to arrange the date of their match within these limits, the *Committee* should announce that the match must be played at a stated time on the last day of the period, unless the players agree to a prior date.

33-4 Handicap Stroke Table

The *Committee* must publish a table indicating the order of holes at which handicap strokes are to be given or received.

33-5 Score Card

In stroke play, the *Committee* must provide each *competitor* with a score card containing the date and the *competitor's* name or, in *foursome* or *four-ball* stroke play, the *competitors'* names.

In stroke play, the Committee is responsible for the addition of scores and application of the handicap recorded on the score card.

In *four-ball* stroke play, the *Committee* is responsible for recording the better-ball score for each hole and in the process applying the handicaps recorded on the score card, and adding the better-ball scores.

In bogey, par and Stableford competitions, the *Committee* is responsible for applying the handicap recorded on the score card and determining the result of each hole and the overall result or points total.

Note | The *Committee* may request that each *competitor* records the date and his name on his score card.

33-6 Decision of Ties

The *Committee* must announce the manner, day and time for the decision of a halved match or of a tie, whether played on level terms or under handicap.

A halved match must not be decided by stroke play. A tie in stroke play must not be decided by a match.

33-7   **Disqualification Penalty; Committee Discretion**

A penalty of disqualification may in exceptional individual cases be waived, modified or imposed if the *Committee* considers such action warranted.

Any penalty less than disqualification must not be waived or modified.

If a *Committee* considers that a player is guilty of a serious breach of etiquette, it may impose a penalty of disqualification under this Rule.

33-8   **Local Rules**

33-8 a   **Policy**

The *Committee* may establish Local Rules for local abnormal conditions if they are consistent with the policy set forth in Appendix I.

33-8 b   **Waiving or Modifying a Rule**

A Rule of Golf must not be waived by a Local Rule. However, if a *Committee* considers that local abnormal conditions interfere with the proper playing of the game to the extent that it is necessary to make a Local Rule that modifies the Rules of Golf, the Local Rule must be authorised by the *R&A*.

RULE **33**

INCIDENTS

In the third round of the 2000 Weetabix Women's British Open Championship at Royal Birkdale Golf Club, Karrie Webb took incorrect relief from a fixed sprinkler head on her line of play.

Webb was entitled to relief from the fixed sprinkler head within two club-lengths of the putting green by a Local Rule and together with her fellow-competitor, Trish Johnson, Webb referred to the wording of the Local Rule contained in Appendix I of the Rules of Golf. Having read the Local Rule, Webb confirmed that she was entitled to relief. She determined her nearest point of relief but then mistakenly measured a one club-length area within which to drop the ball. Webb was required to drop at the nearest point of relief and having dropped and played the ball from within one club-length of this point rather than at it, Webb was in breach of the Local Rule and incurred a penalty of two strokes.

Rules officials in the Championship office noticed the infringement on the television coverage but could not prevent the breach occurring. Webb was advised of the infringement and resulting penalty at the conclusion of her round but before she signed her score card, thereby avoiding a disqualification for signing for a score lower than actually taken.

The importance of Rule 33-6, that is of establishing a method of settling ties prior to a stroke-play competition, was emphasised at the 2006 Women's World Amateur Team Championship held in Stellenbosch, South Africa. The biennial Championships involve three-player teams playing four days of stroke play, with the best two scores counting each day. Due to daylight constraints, a team play-off was not feasible and, consequently, it was necessary for the Committee to establish a method of breaking a tie for first place should one occur.

At the conclusion of the Championship, the women's teams from Sweden and South Africa were tied on 10 under par, and this brought the tie-breaking method into play. The first criteria for determining the order if two or more teams were tied for first place was to take into account the non-counting score for the final round. However, the non-counting scores on the last day for Sweden and South Africa were 75 and, therefore, the second criteria of the non-counting score on the third day had to be relied upon. With South Africa's non-counting score on the third day being a 73 to Sweden's 77, the South African women were crowned champions. This highlighted the importance of having a full-proof method of settling a tie.

FAQ

Q Can a player be disqualified for an omission or error in adding his score or Stableford points on his score card?

A A competitor is responsible only for the correctness of the score recorded for each hole (Rule 6-6d) and the Committee is responsible for the addition of scores or points (Rule 33-5). If a total recorded by a competitor is incorrect, it is the responsibility of the Committee to correct the error, without penalty to the competitor.

Q Can I use a motorised cart?

A Unless the use of a motorised cart is prohibited by the Committee in the conditions of competition (Rule 33-1), a player may use such equipment during a competition.

It was only after the exceptional consideration of South Africa's and Sweden's non-counting team scores on the third day of play that officials were able to declare South Africa the winners of the 2006 Women's World Amateur Team Championship.

It is a policy of The R&A to encourage golfers with physical difficulties to play the game if at all possible. However, it is important that Clubs and Committees consider the issues surrounding the use of golf carts and any relevant legislation, as well as health and safety issues, weather and ground conditions. They should also decide whether the layout of the course dictates that the use of carts is impracticable.

If a Club or Committee does decide to permit the use of golf carts in competition, they may wish to consider putting restrictions on their use: for example, that golf carts would be permitted only for competitors with medical certificates or for competitors over a certain age who would otherwise be unable to participate due to physical limitations as a result of their age.

It is a matter for individual Clubs and Committees to decide and to be separately advised as to their legal position. It would be sensible for Clubs to ensure that they are aware of the relevant disability discrimination issues and of any guidance given by the Government or related bodies.

If a Club permits the use of golf carts, it would be prudent to ensure that appropriate insurance cover is in operation in the event of any accident or personal injury occurring as a result of their use.

RULE 34 — DISPUTES AND DECISIONS

Definitions

All defined terms are in *italics* and are listed alphabetically in the Definitions section – see pages 13–24.

34-1 Claims and Penalties

34-1 a   Match Play

If a claim is lodged with the *Committee* under Rule 2-5, a decision should be given as soon as possible so that the state of the match may, if necessary, be adjusted. If a claim is not made in accordance with Rule 2-5, it must not be considered by the *Committee*.

There is no time limit on applying the disqualification penalty for a breach of Rule 1-3.

34-1 b   Stroke Play

In stroke play, a penalty must not be rescinded, modified or imposed after the competition has closed. A competition is closed when the result has been officially announced or, in stroke play qualifying followed by match play, when the player has teed off in his first match.

Exceptions

A penalty of disqualification must be imposed after the competition has closed if a *competitor*:

(i) was in breach of Rule 1-3 (Agreement to Waive Rules); or

(ii) returned a score card on which he had recorded a handicap that, before the competition closed, he knew was higher than that to which he was entitled, and this affected the number of strokes received (Rule 6-2b); or

(iii) returned a score for any hole lower than actually taken (Rule 6-6d) for any reason other than failure to include a penalty that, before the competition closed, he did not know he had incurred; or

(iv) knew, before the competition closed, that he had been in breach of any other *Rule* for which the penalty is disqualification.

34-2   **Referee's Decision**

If a *referee* has been appointed by the *Committee*, his decision is final.

34-3   **Committee's Decision**

In the absence of a *referee*, any dispute or doubtful point on the *Rules* must be referred to the *Committee*, whose decision is final.

If the *Committee* cannot come to a decision, it may refer the dispute or doubtful point to the Rules of Golf Committee of the R&A, whose decision is final.

If the dispute or doubtful point has not been referred to the Rules of Golf Committee, the player or players may request that an agreed statement be referred through a duly authorised representative of the *Committee* to the Rules of Golf Committee for an opinion as to the correctness of the decision given. The reply will be sent to this authorised representative.

If play is conducted other than in accordance with the Rules of Golf, the Rules of Golf Committee will not give a decision on any question.

RULE **34**

INCIDENTS

The 2004 Open Championship featured an incident that emphasised the importance of timing in terms of discovering a possible breach of the Rules. At the 14th hole on the final day, eventual winner Todd Hamilton putted to a few feet from the hole. When he marked and lifted his ball, he tapped his ball-marker down three times with his ball, replaced the ball and holed the putt.

Hamilton was already involved in the first hole of his four-hole play-off with Ernie Els when a television viewer made contact with The R&A Rules Office at the Championship and advised that he thought he had seen Hamilton touch his line of putt in breach of Rule 16-1a on the 14th hole.

As any such reports have to be followed up, the footage of the incident was closely reviewed. Had Hamilton breached Rule 16-1a, he would have been liable to a penalty of two strokes at the 14th hole. However, as he had returned his score card for that round – without any penalty included for that hole – and the competition had not yet closed (see Rule 34-1b), he would have been subject to a penalty of disqualification for returning a score for a hole lower than had actually been taken, in breach of Rule 6-6d. A further twist was that, had there been a breach but it had not come to light until after the competition was closed, in view of Rule 34-1b, which provides that no penalty can be waived, modified or imposed after a competition has closed, there would have been no penalty.

As it transpired, the replays confirmed that Hamilton had not breached the Rules at the 14th hole, and the American went on to defeat Ernie Els and lift the Claret Jug.

FAQ

Q What are the Rules for Greensomes and Texas Scrambles?

A These are not recognised forms of play and thus are not covered by the Rules of Golf. Therefore, it is a matter for the Committee in charge of the competition to decide upon any matters that may arise and its decision shall be final (Rule 34-3).

Q When is a record score officially recognised as a "course record"?

A The term "course record" is not defined in the Rules of Golf. Therefore it is a matter for the Committee in charge of the competition to decide whether it recognises a score as a course record.

It is recommended that a record score should be recognised only if made in an individual stroke-play competition (excluding a Stableford or a par/bogey competition) with the holes and tee-markers in their championship positions and when a Local Rule on preferred lies is not in operation.

While Todd Hamilton was in the course of his four-hole play-off against Ernie Els for the Claret Jug, a possible Rules infringement on the 14th hole was lodged against him with The R&A Rules Office at Royal Troon. Fortunately for Hamilton it was not upheld, and he went on to become The Open winner for 2004.

APPENDIX I

Contents

APPENDIX I – LOCAL RULES; CONDITIONS OF COMPETITION

Definitions

All defined terms are in *italics* and are listed alphabetically in the Definitions section – see pages 13–24.

PART A LOCAL RULES

As provided in Rule 33-8a, the *Committee* may make and publish Local Rules for local abnormal conditions if they are consistent with the policy established in this Appendix. In addition, detailed information regarding acceptable and prohibited Local Rules is provided in "Decisions on the Rules of Golf" under Rule 33-8 and in "Guidance on Running a Competition".

If local abnormal conditions interfere with the proper playing of the game and the *Committee* considers it necessary to modify a Rule of Golf, authorisation from the *R&A* must be obtained.

1 Defining Bounds and Margins

Specifying means used to define *out of bounds*, *water hazards*, *lateral water hazards*, *ground under repair*, *obstructions* and integral parts of the *course* (Rule 33-2a).

2 Water Hazards
a Lateral Water Hazards

Clarifying the status of *water hazards* that may be *lateral water hazards* (Rule 26).

b Ball Played Provisionally Under Rule 26-1

Permitting play of a ball provisionally under Rule 26-1 for a ball that may be in a *water hazard* (including a *lateral water hazard*) of such character that, if the original ball is not found, it is known or virtually certain that it is in the *water hazard* and it would be impracticable to determine whether the ball is in the *hazard* or to do so would unduly delay play.

3 Areas of the Course Requiring Preservation; Environmentally-Sensitive Areas

Assisting preservation of the *course* by defining areas, including turf nurseries, young plantations and other parts of the *course* under cultivation, as *ground under repair* from which play is prohibited.

When the *Committee* is required to prohibit play from environmentally-sensitive areas that are on or adjoin the *course*, it should make a Local Rule clarifying the relief procedure.

4 Course Conditions – Mud, Extreme Wetness, Poor Conditions and Protection of Course
a Lifting an Embedded Ball, Cleaning

Temporary conditions that might interfere with proper playing of the game, including mud and extreme wetness, warranting relief for an embedded ball anywhere *through the green* or permitting lifting, cleaning and replacing a ball anywhere *through the green* or on a closely-mown area *through the green*.

b "Preferred Lies" and "Winter Rules"

Adverse conditions, including the poor condition of the *course* or the existence of mud, are sometimes so general, particularly during winter months, that the *Committee* may decide to grant relief by temporary Local Rule either to protect the *course* or to promote fair and pleasant play. The Local Rule should be withdrawn as soon as the conditions warrant.

5 Obstructions
a General

Clarifying status of objects that may be *obstructions* (Rule 24).

Declaring any construction to be an integral part of the *course* and, accordingly, not an *obstruction*, e.g., built-up sides of *teeing grounds*, *putting greens* and *bunkers* (Rules 24 and 33-2a).

b Stones in Bunkers

Allowing the removal of stones in *bunkers* by declaring them to be movable *obstructions* (Rule 24-1).

c Roads and Paths

(i) Declaring artificial surfaces and sides of roads and paths to be integral parts of the *course*, or

(ii) Providing relief of the type afforded under Rule 24-2b from roads and paths not having artificial surfaces and sides if they could unfairly affect play.

d Immovable Obstructions Close to Putting Green

Providing relief from intervention by immovable *obstructions* on or within two club-lengths of the *putting green* when the ball lies within two club-lengths of the immovable *obstruction*.

e Protection of Young Trees

Providing relief for the protection of young trees.

f Temporary Obstructions

Providing relief from interference by temporary *obstructions* (e.g., grandstands, television cables and equipment, etc).

6 Dropping Zones

Establishing special areas on which balls may or must be dropped when it is not feasible or practicable to proceed exactly in conformity with Rule 24-2b or 24-3 (Immovable Obstruction), Rule 25-1b or 25-1c (Abnormal Ground Conditions), Rule 25-3 (Wrong Putting Green), Rule 26-1 (Water Hazards and Lateral Water Hazards) or Rule 28 (Ball Unplayable).

PART B SPECIMEN LOCAL RULES

Within the policy established in Part A of this Appendix, the *Committee* may adopt a Specimen Local Rule by referring, on a score card or notice board, to the examples given below. However, Specimen Local Rules of a temporary nature should not be printed on a score card.

1 Water Hazards, Ball Played Provisionally Under Rule 26-1

If a *water hazard* (including a *lateral water hazard*) is of such size and shape and/or located in such a position that:

(i) it would be impracticable to determine whether the ball is in the *hazard* or to do so would unduly delay play, and

(ii) if the original ball is not found, it is known or virtually certain that it is in the *water hazard*,

the *Committee* may introduce a Local Rule permitting the play of a ball provisionally under Rule 26-1. The ball is played provisionally under any of the applicable options under Rule 26-1 or any applicable Local Rule. In such a case, if a ball is played provisionally and the original ball is in a *water hazard*, the player may play the original ball as it lies or continue with the ball played provisionally, but he may not proceed under Rule 26-1 with regard to the original ball.

In these circumstances, **the following Local Rule is recommended**:

"If there is doubt whether a ball is in or is *lost* in the *water hazard* (specify location), the player may play another ball provisionally under any of the applicable options in Rule 26-1.

If the original ball is found outside the *water hazard*, the player must continue play with it.

If the original ball is found in the *water hazard*, the player may either play the original ball as it lies or continue with the ball played provisionally under Rule 26-1.

If the original ball is not found or identified within the five-minute search period, the player must continue with the ball played provisionally.

PENALTY FOR BREACH OF LOCAL RULE:
Match Play – Loss of hole;
Stroke Play – Two strokes."

2 Areas of the Course Requiring Preservation; Environmentally – Sensitive Areas

a Ground Under Repair; Play Prohibited

If the *Committee* wishes to protect any area of the *course*, it should declare it to be *ground under repair* and prohibit play from within that area. **The following Local Rule is recommended:**

"The _____(defined by _____) is *ground under repair* from which play is prohibited. If a player's ball lies in the area, or if it interferes with the player's *stance* or the area of his intended swing, the player must take relief under Rule 25-1.

PENALTY FOR BREACH OF LOCAL RULE:
Match play – Loss of hole;
Stroke play – Two strokes."

b Environmentally-Sensitive Areas

If an appropriate authority (i.e. a Government Agency or the like) prohibits entry into and/or play from an area on or adjoining the *course* for environmental reasons, the *Committee* should make a Local Rule clarifying the relief procedure.

The *Committee* has some discretion in terms of whether the area is defined as *ground under repair*, a *water hazard* or *out of bounds*. However, it may not simply define the area to be a *water hazard* if it does not meet the Definition of a *"Water Hazard"* and it should attempt to preserve the character of the hole.

The following Local Rule is recommended:
"I Definition
An environmentally-sensitive area (ESA) is an area so declared by an appropriate authority, entry into and/or play from which is prohibited for environmental reasons. These areas may be defined as *ground under repair,* a *water hazard*, a *lateral water hazard* or *out of bounds* at the discretion of the *Committee*, provided that in the case of an ESA that has been defined as a *water hazard* or a *lateral water hazard*, the area is, by definition, a *water hazard*.

Note: The *Committee* may not declare an area to be environmentally-sensitive.

II Ball in Environmentally-Sensitive Area
a Ground Under Repair

If a ball is in an ESA is defined as *ground under repair*, a ball must be dropped in accordance with Rule 25-1b.

If it is known or virtually certain that a ball that has not been found is in an ESA defined as *ground under repair*, the player may take relief without penalty as prescribed in Rule 25-1c.

b Water Hazards and Lateral Water Hazards

If it is known or virtually certain that a ball that has not been found is in an ESA defined as a *water hazard* or *lateral water hazard*, the player must, under penalty of one stroke, proceed under Rule 26-1.

Note: If a ball, dropped in accordance with Rule 26 rolls into a position where the ESA interferes with the player's *stance* or the area of his intended swing, the player must take relief as provided in Clause III of this Local Rule.

c Out of Bounds

If a ball is in an ESA defined as *out of bounds*, the player must play a ball, under penalty of one stroke, as nearly as possible at the spot from which the original ball was last played (see Rule 20-5).

III Interference with Stance or Area of Intended Swing

Interference by an ESA occurs when the ESA interferes with the player's *stance* or the area of his intended swing. If interference exists, the player must take relief as follows:
(a) Through the Green: If the ball lies *through the green*, the point on the *course* nearest to where the ball lies must be determined that **(a)** is not nearer the *hole*, **(b)** avoids interference

Relief from staked trees

The staked tree interferes with my swing. I must take relief according to the Local Rules, but my nearest point of relief leaves me blocked by the big tree.

I am afraid that is just bad luck. You must drop your ball within one club-length of the nearest point of relief.

by the ESA and (**c**) is not in a *hazard* or on a *putting green*. The player must lift the ball and drop it, without penalty, within one club-length of the point so determined on a part of the *course* that fulfils (**a**), (**b**) and (**c**) above.

(**b**) **In a Hazard:** If the ball is in a *hazard*, the player must lift the ball and drop it either:

(**i**) Without penalty, in the *hazard*, as near as possible to the spot where the ball lay, but not nearer the *hole*, on a part of the *course* that provides complete relief from the ESA; or

(**ii**) Under penalty of one stroke, outside the *hazard*, keeping the point where the ball lay directly between the *hole* and the spot on which the ball is dropped, with no limit to how far behind the *hazard* the ball may be dropped. Additionally, the player may proceed under Rule 26 or 28 if applicable.

(**c**) **On the Putting Green:** If the ball lies on the *putting green*, the player must lift the ball and place it, without penalty, in the nearest position to where it lay that affords complete relief from the ESA, but not nearer the *hole* or in a *hazard*.

The ball may be cleaned when lifted under Clause III of this Local Rule.

Exception: A player may not take relief under Clause III of this Local Rule if (**a**) it is clearly unreasonable for him to make a *stroke* because of interference by anything other than an ESA or (**b**) interference by an ESA would occur only through use of an unnecessarily abnormal *stance*, swing or direction of play.

PENALTY FOR BREACH OF LOCAL RULE:
Match play – Loss of hole;
Stroke play – Two strokes.

Note: In the case of a serious breach of this Local Rule, the *Committee* may impose a penalty of disqualification."

3 Protection of Young Trees

When it is desired to prevent damage to young trees, **the following Local Rule is recommended:**

"Protection of young trees identified by _____. If such a tree interferes with a player's *stance* or the area of his intended swing, the ball must be lifted, without penalty, and dropped in accordance with the procedure prescribed in Rule 24-2b (Immovable *Obstruction*). If the ball lies in a *water hazard*, the player must lift and drop the ball in accordance with Rule 24-2b(i), except that the *nearest point of relief* must be in the *water hazard* and the ball must be dropped in the *water hazard* or the player may proceed under Rule 26. The ball may be cleaned when lifted under this Local Rule.

Exception: A player may not obtain relief under this Local Rule if (**a**) it is clearly unreasonable for him to make a *stroke* because of interference by anything other than the tree or (**b**) interference by the tree would occur only through use of an unnecessarily abnormal *stance*, swing or direction of play.

PENALTY FOR BREACH OF LOCAL RULE:
Match play – Loss of hole;
Stroke play – Two strokes."

4 Course Conditions – Mud, Extreme Wetness, Poor Conditions and Protection of the Course

a Relief for Embedded Ball

Rule 25-2 provides relief, without penalty, for a ball embedded in its own pitch-mark in any closely-mown area *through the green*. On the *putting green*, a ball may be lifted and damage caused by the impact of a ball may be repaired (Rules 16-1b and c). When permission to take relief for an embedded ball anywhere *through the green* would be warranted, **the following Local Rule is recommended:**

"*Through the green*, a ball that is embedded in its own pitch-mark in the ground may be lifted, without penalty, cleaned and dropped as near as possible to where it lay but not nearer the *hole*. The ball when dropped must first strike a part of the *course through the green*.

Exception 1: A player may not take relief under this Local Rule if the ball is embedded in sand in an area that is not closely mown.
Exception 2: A player may not take relief under this Local Rule if it is clearly unreasonable for him to make a *stroke* because of interference by anything other than the condition covered by this Local Rule.

PENALTY FOR BREACH OF LOCAL RULE:
Match play – Loss of hole;
Stroke play – Two strokes."

b Cleaning Ball

Conditions, such as extreme wetness causing significant amounts of mud to adhere to the ball, may be such that permission to lift, clean and replace the ball would be appropriate. In these circumstances, **the following Local Rule is recommended:**

"(Specify area) a ball may be lifted, cleaned and replaced without penalty.

Note: The position of the ball must be marked before it is lifted under this Local Rule – see Rule 20-1.

PENALTY FOR BREACH OF LOCAL RULE:
Match play – Loss of hole;
Stroke play – Two strokes."

c "Preferred Lies" and "Winter Rules"

Ground under repair is provided for in Rule 25 and occasional local abnormal conditions that might interfere with fair play and are not widespread should be defined as *ground under repair*.

However, adverse conditions, such as heavy snows, spring thaws, prolonged rains or extreme heat can make fairways unsatisfactory and sometimes prevent use of heavy mowing equipment. When such conditions are so general throughout a *course* that the *Committee* believes "preferred lies" or "winter rules" would promote fair play or help protect the *course*, **the following Local Rule is recommended:**

"A ball lying on a closely-mown area *through the green* [or specify a more restricted area, e.g. at the 6th hole] may be lifted, without penalty, and cleaned. Before lifting the ball, the player must mark its position. Having lifted the ball, he must place it on a spot within [specify area, e.g. six inches, one club-length, etc.] of and not nearer the *hole* than where it originally lay, that is not in a *hazard* and not on a *putting green*.

A player may place his ball only once, and it is *in play* when it has been placed (Rule 20-4). If the ball fails to come to rest on the spot on which it is placed, Rule 20-3d applies. If the ball when placed comes to rest on the spot on which it is placed and it subsequently *moves*, there is no penalty and the ball must be played as it lies, unless the provisions of any other *Rule* apply.

If the player fails to mark the position of the ball before lifting it or *moves* the ball in any other manner, such as rolling it with a club, he incurs a penalty of one stroke.

Note: "Closely-mown area" means any area of the *course,* including paths through the rough, cut to fairway height or less.

*PENALTY FOR BREACH OF LOCAL RULE:

Match play – Loss of hole;
Stroke play – Two strokes.
*If a player incurs the general penalty for a breach of this Local Rule, no additional penalty under the Local Rule is applied."

d Aeration Holes

When a *course* has been aerated, a Local Rule permitting relief, without penalty, from an aeration hole may be warranted. **The following Local Rule is recommended:**

"*Through the green,* a ball that comes to rest in or on an aeration hole may be lifted, without penalty, cleaned and dropped, as near as possible to the spot where it lay but not nearer the *hole.* The ball when dropped must first strike a part of the *course through the green.*

On the *putting green,* a ball that comes to rest in or on an aeration hole may be placed at the nearest spot not nearer the *hole* that avoids the situation.

PENALTY FOR BREACH OF LOCAL RULE:
Match play – Loss of hole;
Stroke play – Two strokes."

e Seams of Cut Turf

If a *Committee* wishes to allow relief from seams of cut turf, but not from the cut turf itself, **the following Local Rule is recommended:**

"*Through the green,* seams of cut turf (not the turf itself) are deemed to be *ground under repair.* However, interference by a seam with the player's *stance* is deemed not to be, of itself, interference under Rule 25-1. If the ball lies in or touches the seam or the seam interferes with the area of intended swing, relief is available under Rule 25-1. All seams within the cut turf area are considered the same seam."

PENALTY FOR BREACH OF LOCAL RULE:
Match play – Loss of hole;
Stroke play – Two strokes."

5 Stones in Bunkers

Stones are, by definition, *loose impediments* and, when a player's ball is in a *hazard,* a stone lying in or touching the *hazard* may not be touched or moved (Rule 13-4). However, stones in *bunkers* may represent a danger to players (a player could be injured by a stone struck by the player's club in an attempt to play the ball) and they may interfere with the proper playing of the game.

When permission to lift a stone in a *bunker* is warranted, **the following Local Rule is recommended:**

"Stones in *bunkers* are movable *obstructions* (Rule 24-1 applies)."

6 Immovable Obstructions Close to Putting Green

Rule 24-2 provides relief, without penalty, from interference by an immovable *obstruction,* but it also provides that, except on the *putting green,* intervention on the *line of play* is not, of itself, interference under this Rule.

However, on some courses, the aprons of the *putting greens* are so closely mown that players may wish to putt from just off the green. In such conditions, immovable *obstructions* on the

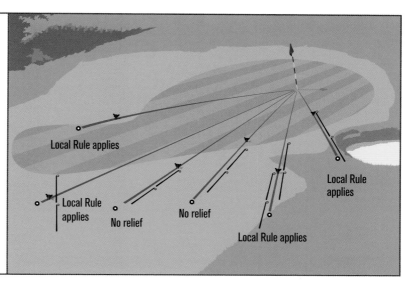

A player is entitled to relief from an immovable obstruction under Rule 24-2. If the specimen Local Rule is introduced, a player is also entitled to relief for intervention to his line of play provided:

(a) the immovable obstruction is on or within two club-lengths of the putting green; and
(b) the ball lies within two club-lengths of the immovable obstruction.
(c) the ball lies on the putting green and the immovable obstruction within two club-lengths of the putting green intervenes on his line of play.

apron may interfere with the proper playing of the game and the introduction of **the following Local Rule providing additional relief, without penalty, from intervention by an immovable *obstruction* would be warranted:**

"Relief from interference by an immovable *obstruction* may be obtained under Rule 24-2. In addition, if a ball lies off the *putting green* but not in a *hazard* and an immovable *obstruction* on or within two club-lengths of the *putting green* and within two club-lengths of the ball intervenes on the *line of play* between the ball and the *hole*, the player may take relief as follows:

The ball must be lifted and dropped at the nearest point to where the ball lay that **(a)** is not nearer the *hole*, **(b)** avoids intervention and **(c)** is not in a *hazard* or on a *putting green*. The ball may be cleaned when lifted.

Relief under this Local Rule is also available if the player's ball lies on the *putting green* and an immovable *obstruction* within two club-lengths of the *putting green* intervenes on his *line of putt*. The player may take relief as follows:

The ball must be lifted and placed at the nearest point to where the ball lay that **(a)** is not nearer the *hole*, **(b)** avoids intervention and **(c)** is not in a *hazard*. The ball may be cleaned when lifted.

PENALTY FOR BREACH OF LOCAL RULE:
Match play – Loss of hole;
Stroke play – Two strokes."

APPENDIX I Incident

A Local Rule that is frequently introduced at events played on links courses, relates to immovable obstructions close to the putting green, the most common example of such immovable obstructions being fixed sprinkler heads.

The Local Rule provides additional relief to that found in the Rules of Golf, by enabling a player, whose ball lies off the putting green but not in a hazard, to take a drop if an obstruction, which lies within two club-lengths of the putting green, is within two club-lengths of the player's ball and also on his line of play. When taking relief, the player must drop his ball at the nearest point where there is no intervention from the obstruction, which is not in a hazard and not on a putting green. It is important to note that there is not a one club-length dropping area, as is normally the case when free relief is given from an immovable obstruction, although the ball, when dropped, can roll up to two club-lengths without a re-drop being required (Rule 20-2c).

Tiger Woods at the 2004 Open Championship drops his ball when taking relief under the Local Rule for immovable obstructions close to the putting green.

The introduction of this Local Rule is appropriate on courses where players may frequently elect to putt from off the green and, consequently, the Local Rule was in place during The Open Championship at Royal Troon in 2004.

In the final round, Tiger Woods utilised the Local Rule when his ball lay close to the 18th green. However, matters were complicated when, in dropping the ball at the nearest point of relief, the ball rolled into a bunker. In this situation, Rule 20-2c (ii) comes into play and the player is required to re-drop the ball. Tiger did so and the same thing happened. Rule 20-2c then provides that the ball must be placed as near as possible to the spot where it first struck the course when re-dropped.

7 Temporary Obstructions

When temporary obstructions are installed on or adjoining the course, the *Committee* should define the status of such obstructions as movable, immovable or temporary immovable obstructions.

a Temporary Immovable Obstructions

If the *Committee* defines such obstructions as temporary immovable obstructions, **the following Local Rule is recommended:**

"**I Definition**

A temporary immovable obstructions (TIO) is a non-permanent artificial object that is often erected in conjunction with a competition and is fixed or not readily movable.

Examples of TIOs include, but are not limited to, tents, scoreboards, grandstands, television towers and lavatories.

Supporting guy wires are part of the TIO, unless the *Committee* declares that they are to be treated as elevated power lines or cables.

II Interference

Interference by a TIO occurs when (**a**) the ball lies in front of and so close to the TIO that the TIO interferes with the player's *stance* or the area of his intended swing, or (**b**) the ball lies in, on, under or behind the TIO so that any part of the TIO intervenes directly between the player's ball and the *hole* and is on his *line of play*; interference also exists if the ball lies within one club-length of a spot equidistant from the *hole* where such intervention would exist.

Note: A ball is under a TIO when it is below the outer most edges of the TIO, even if these edges do not extend downwards to the ground.

III Relief

A player may obtain relief from interference by a TIO, including a TIO that is *out of bounds*, as follows:

(**a**) **Through the Green:** If the ball lies *through the green*, the point on the *course* nearest to where the ball lies must be determined that (**a**) is not nearer the *hole*, (**b**) avoids interference as defined in Clause II and (**c**) is not in a *hazard* or on a *putting green*. The player must lift the ball and drop it, without penalty, within one club-length of the point so determined on a part of the *course* that fulfils (**a**), (**b**) and (**c**) above.

(**b**) **In a Hazard:** If the ball is in a *hazard,* the player must lift and drop the ball either:

(**i**) Without penalty, in accordance with Clause III(a) above, except that the nearest part of the *course* affording complete relief must be in the *hazard* and the ball must be dropped in the *hazard* or, if complete relief is impossible, on a part of the *course* within the *hazard* that affords maximum available relief; or

(**ii**) Under penalty of one stroke, outside the *hazard* as follows: the point on the *course* nearest to where the ball lies must be determined that (**a**) is not nearer the *hole,* (**b**) avoids interference as defined in Clause II and (**c**) is not in a *hazard*. The player must drop the ball within one club-length of the point so determined on a part of the *course* that fulfils (**a**), (**b**) and (**c**) above.

The ball may be cleaned when lifted under Clause III.

Note 1: If the ball lies in a *hazard*, nothing in this Local Rule precludes the player from proceeding under Rule 26 or Rule 28, if applicable.

Note 2: If a ball to be dropped under this Local Rule is not immediately recoverable, another ball may be *substituted*.

Note 3: A *Committee* may make a Local Rule (**a**) permitting or requiring a player to use a dropping zone when taking relief from a TIO or (**b**) permitting a player, as an additional relief option, to drop the ball on the opposite side of the TIO from the point established under Clause III, but otherwise in accordance with Clause III.

Exceptions: If a player's ball lies in front of or behind the TIO (not in, on or under the TIO), he may not obtain relief under Clause III if:

1 It is clearly unreasonable for him to make a *stroke* or, in the case of intervention, to make a *stroke* such that the ball could finish on a direct line to the *hole*, because of interference by anything other than the TIO;

2 Interference by the TIO would occur only through use of an unnecessarily abnormal *stance,* swing or direction of play; or

3 In the case of intervention, it would be clearly unreasonable to expect the player to be able to strike the ball far enough towards the *hole* to reach the TIO.

A player not entitled to relief due to these exceptions may proceed under Rule 24-2, if applicable.

IV Ball in TIO Not Found

If it is known or virtually certain that a ball that has not been found is in, on or under a TIO, a ball may be dropped under the provisions of Clause III or Clause V, if applicable. For the purpose of applying Clauses III and V, the ball is deemed to lie at the spot where it last crossed the outermost limits of the TIO (Rule 24-3).

V Dropping Zones

If the player has interference from a TIO, the *Committee* may permit or require the use of a dropping zone. If the player uses a dropping zone in taking relief, he must drop the ball in the dropping zone nearest to where his ball originally lay or is deemed to lie under Clause IV (even though the nearest dropping zone may be nearer the *hole*).

Note: A *Committee* may make a Local Rule prohibiting the use of a dropping zone that is nearer the *hole*.

PENALTY FOR BREACH OF LOCAL RULE:
Match play – Loss of hole;
Stroke play – Two strokes."

b Temporary Power Lines and Cables

When temporary power lines, cables, or telephone lines are installed on the *course*, **the following Local Rule is recommended:**

"Temporary power lines, cables, telephone lines and mats covering or stanchions supporting them are *obstructions*:

If there are temporary immovable obstructions, such as TV towers, on the course, the Committee should introduce a Local Rule providing for relief from such temporary immovable obstructions.

1 If they are readily movable, Rule 24-1 applies.
2 If they are fixed or not readily movable, the player may, if the ball lies *through the green* or in a *bunker*, obtain relief as provided in Rule 24-2b. If the ball lies in a *water hazard*, the player may lift and drop the ball in accordance with Rule 24-2b(i) except that the *nearest point of relief* must be in the *water hazard* and the ball must be dropped in the *water hazard* or the player may proceed under Rule 26.
3 If a ball strikes an elevated power line or cable, the *stroke* must be cancelled and replayed, without penalty (see Rule 20-5). If the ball is not immediately recoverable another ball may be *substituted*.

Note: Guy wires supporting a temporary immovable *obstruction* are part of the temporary immovable *obstruction* unless the *Committee*, by Local Rule, declares that they are to be treated as elevated power lines or cables.

Exception: A *stroke* that results in a ball striking an elevated junction section of cable rising from the ground must not be replayed.

---

4 Grass-covered cable trenches are *ground under repair,* even if not marked, and Rule 25-1b applies."

8 Dropping Zones

If the *Committee* considers that it is not feasible or practicable to proceed in accordance with a Rule providing relief, it may establish dropping zones in which balls may or must be dropped when taking relief. Generally, such dropping zones should be provided as an additional relief option to those available under the Rule itself, rather than being mandatory.

Using the example of a dropping zone for a *water hazard*, when such a dropping zone is established, **the following Local Rule is recommended:**

"If a ball is in or it is known or virtually certain that a ball that has not been found is in the *water hazard* (specify location), the player may:

(**i**) proceed under Rule 26; or
(**ii**) as an additional option, drop a ball, under penalty of one stroke, in the dropping zone.

PENALTY FOR BREACH OF LOCAL RULE:
Match play – Loss of hole;
Stroke play – Two strokes."

Note: When using a dropping zone the following provisions apply regarding the dropping and re-dropping of the ball:
(**a**) The player does not have to stand within the dropping zone when dropping the ball.
(**b**) The dropped ball must first strike a part of the *course* within the dropping zone.
(**c**) If the dropping zone is defined by a line, the line is within the dropping zone.
(**d**) The dropped ball does not have to come to rest within the dropping zone.
(**e**) The dropped ball must be re-dropped if it rolls and comes to rest in a position covered by Rule 20-2c(i-vi).
(**f**) The dropped ball may roll nearer the *hole* than the spot where it first struck a part of the course provided it comes to rest within two club-lengths of that spot and not into any of the positions covered by (e).
(**g**) Subject to the provisions of (e) and (f), the dropped ball may roll and come to rest nearer the *hole* than:
• its original position or estimated position (see Rule 20-2b);
• the *nearest point of relief* or maximum available relief (Rule 24-2, 24-3, 25-1 or 25-3); or
• the point where the original ball last crossed the margin of the *water hazard* or *lateral water hazard* (Rule 26-1).

9 Distance-Measuring Devices

If the *Committee* wishes to act in accordance with the Note under Rule 14-3, **the following wording is recommended:**

"[Specify as appropriate, e.g. In this competition, or For all play at this course, etc.], a player may obtain distance information by using a device that measures distance only. If, during a *stipulated round*, a player uses a distance-measuring device that is designed to gauge or measure other conditions that might affect his play (e.g. gradient, windspeed, temperature, etc.), the player is in breach of Rule 14-3, for which the penalty is disqualification, regardless of whether any such additional function is actually used."

PART C CONDITIONS OF THE COMPETITION

Rule 33-1 provides, "The *Committee* must establish the conditions under which a competition is to be played." The conditions should include many matters such as method of entry, eligibility, number of rounds to be played, etc. which it is not appropriate to deal with in the Rules of Golf or this Appendix. Detailed information regarding these conditions is provided in "Decisions on the Rules of Golf" under Rule 33-1 and in "Guidance on Running a Competition".

However, there are a number of matters that might be covered in the Conditions of the Competition to which the *Committee's* attention is specifically drawn. These are:

1 Specification of Clubs and Balls

The following conditions are recommended only for competitions involving expert players:

a List of Conforming Driver Heads

On its web site (www.randa.org) the *R&A* periodically issues a List of Conforming Driver Heads that lists driving clubheads that have been evaluated and found to conform with the Rules of Golf. If the *Committee* wishes to limit players to drivers that have a clubhead, identified by model and loft, that is on the List, the List should be made available and **the following condition of competition used:**

"Any driver the player carries must have a clubhead, identified by model and loft, that is named on the current List of Conforming Driver Heads issued by the *R&A*.

Exception: A driver with a clubhead that was manufactured prior to 1999 is exempt from this condition.

*PENALTY FOR CARRYING, BUT NOT MAKING STROKE WITH, CLUB OR CLUBS IN BREACH OF CONDITION:

Match play – At the conclusion of the hole at which the breach is discovered, the state of the match is adjusted by deducting one hole for each hole at which a breach occurred; maximum deduction per round – Two holes.

Stroke play – Two strokes for each hole at which any breach occurred; maximum penalty per round – Four strokes.

Match or Stroke play – In the event of a breach between the play of two strokes, the penalty applies to the next hole.

Bogey and par competitions – See Note 1 to Rule 32-1a.

Stableford competitions – See Note 1 to Rule 32-1b.

*Any club or clubs carried in breach of this condition must be declared out of play by the player to his opponent in match play or his *marker* or a *fellow-competitor* in stroke play immediately upon discovery that a breach has occurred. If he fails to do so, he is disqualified.

PENALTY FOR MAKING STROKE WITH CLUB IN BREACH OF CONDITION: Disqualification."

b List of Conforming Golf Balls

On its website (www.randa.org) the *R&A* periodically issues a List of Conforming Golf Balls that lists balls that have been tested and found to conform with the Rules of Golf. If the

Committee wishes to require players to play a model of golf ball on the List, the List should be made available and **the following condition of competition used:**

"The ball the player plays must be named on the current List of Conforming Golf Balls issued by the *R&A*.

PENALTY FOR BREACH OF CONDITION: Disqualification."

c One Ball Condition

If it is desired to prohibit changing brands and models of golf balls during a *stipulated round*, **the following condition is recommended:**

"Limitation on Balls Used During Round: (Note to Rule 5-1)

(i) "One Ball" Condition

During a *stipulated round*, the balls a player plays must be of the same brand and model as detailed by a single entry on the current List of Conforming Golf Balls.

Note: If a ball of a different brand and/or model is dropped or placed it may be lifted, without penalty, and the player must then proceed by dropping or placing a proper ball (Rule 20-6).

PENALTY FOR BREACH OF CONDITION:

Match play – At the conclusion of the hole at which the breach is discovered, the state of the match must be adjusted by deducting one hole for each hole at which a breach occurred; maximum deduction per round – Two holes.
Stroke play – Two strokes for each hole at which any breach occurred; maximum penalty per round – Four strokes.

(ii) Procedure When Breach Discovered

When a player discovers that he has played a ball in breach of this condition, he must abandon that ball before playing from the next *teeing ground* and complete the round with a proper ball; otherwise, the player is disqualified. If discovery is made during play of a hole and the player elects to *substitute* a proper ball before completing that hole, the player must place a proper ball on the spot where the ball played in breach of the condition lay."

2 Time of Starting (Note to Rule 6-3a)

If the *Committee* wishes to act in accordance with the Note, **the following wording is recommended:**

"If the player arrives at his starting point, ready to play, within five minutes after his starting time, in the absence of circumstances that warrant waiving the penalty of disqualification as provided in Rule 33-7, the penalty for failure to start on time is loss of the first hole to be played in match play or two strokes in stroke play. Penalty for lateness beyond five minutes is disqualification."

3 Caddie (Note to Rule 6-4)

Rule 6-4 permits a player to use a *caddie* provided he has only one *caddie* at any one time. However, there may be circumstances where a *Committee* may wish to prohibit *caddies* or restrict a player in his choice of *caddie*, e.g. professional golfer, sibling, parent, another player in the competition, etc. In such cases, **the following wording is recommended:**
Use of Caddie Prohibited
"A player is prohibited from using a *caddie* during the *stipulated round*."
Restriction on Who May Serve as Caddie
"A player is prohibited from having
_____ serve as his *caddie* during the *stipulated round*.

PENALTY FOR BREACH OF CONDITION:
Match play – At the conclusion of the hole at which the breach is discovered, the state of the match is adjusted by deducting one hole for each hole at which a breach occurred; maximum deduction per round – Two holes.
Stroke play – Two strokes for each hole at which any breach occurred; maximum penalty per round – Four strokes.

Match or stroke play – In the event of a breach between the play of two holes, the penalty applies to the next hole. A player having a *caddie* in breach of this condition must immediately upon discovery that a breach has occurred ensure that he conforms with this condition for the remainder of the *stipulated round*. Otherwise, the player is disqualified."

4 Pace of Play (Note 2 to Rule 6-7)

The *Committee* may establish pace of play guidelines to help prevent slow play, in accordance with Note 2 to Rule 6-7.

5 Suspension of Play Due to a Dangerous Situation (Note to Rule 6-8b)

As there have been many deaths and injuries from lightning on golf courses, all clubs and sponsors of golf competitions are urged to take precautions for the protection of persons against lightning. Attention is called to Rules 6-8 and 33-2d. If the *Committee* desires to adopt the condition in the Note under Rule 6-8b, **the following wording is recommended:**

"When play is suspended by the *Committee* for a dangerous situation, if the players in a match or group are between the play of two holes, they must not resume play until the *Committee* has ordered a resumption of play. If they are in the process of playing a hole, they must discontinue play immediately and not resume play until the *Committee* has ordered a resumption of play. If a player fails to discontinue play immediately, he is disqualified, unless circumstances warrant waiving the penalty as provided in Rule 33-7.

The signal for suspending play due to a dangerous situation will be a prolonged note of the siren."

The following signals are generally used and it is recommended that all *Committees* do similarly:

Discontinue Play Immediately: One prolonged note of siren.

Discontinue Play: Three consecutive notes of siren, repeated.

Resume Play: Two short notes of siren, repeated.

6 Practice

a General

The *Committee* may make regulations governing practice in accordance with the Note to Rule 7-1, Exception (c) to Rule 7-2, Note 2 to Rule 7 and Rule 33-2c.

b Practice Between Holes (Note 2 to Rule 7)

If the *Committee* wishes to act in accordance with Note 2 to Rule 7-2 **the following wording is recommended:**

"Between the play of two holes, a player must not make any practice *stroke* on or near the *putting green* of the hole last played and must not test the surface of the *putting green* of the hole last played by rolling a ball.

PENALTY FOR BREACH OF CONDITION:

Match play – Loss of next hole.

Stroke play – Two strokes at the next hole.

Match or stroke play – In the case of a breach at the last hole of the *stipulated round*, the player incurs the penalty at that hole."

7 Advice in Team Competitions (Note to Rule 8)

If the *Committee* wishes to act in accordance with the Note under Rule 8, **the following wording is recommended:**

"In accordance with the Note to Rule 8 of the Rules of Golf, each team may appoint one person (in addition to the persons from whom *advice* may be asked under that Rule) who may give *advice* to members of that team. Such person (if it is desired to insert any restriction on who may be nominated insert such restriction here) must be identified to the *Committee* before giving *advice*."

8 New Holes (Note to Rule 33-2b)

The *Committee* may provide, in accordance with the Note to Rule 33-2b, that the *holes* and *teeing grounds* for a single-round competition being held on more than one day may be differently situated on each day.

9 Transportation

If it is desired to require players to walk in a competition, **the following condition is recommended:**

"Players must not ride on any form of transportation during a *stipulated round* unless authorised by the *Committee*.

PENALTY FOR BREACH OF CONDITION:

Match play – At the conclusion of the hole at which the breach is discovered, the state of the match is adjusted by deducting one hole for each hole at which a breach occurred; maximum deduction per round – Two holes.

Stroke play – Two strokes for each hole at which any breach occurred; maximum penalty per round – Four strokes.

Match or stroke play – In the event of a breach between the play of two holes, the penalty applies to the next hole. Use of any unauthorised form of transportation must be discontinued immediately upon discovery that a breach has occurred. Otherwise, the player is disqualified."

10 Anti-Doping

The *Committee* may require, in the conditions of competition, that players comply with an anti-doping policy.

11 How to Decide Ties

In both match play and stroke play, a tie can be an acceptable result. However, when it is desired to have a sole winner, the *Committee* has the authority, under Rule 33-6, to determine how and when a tie is decided. The decision should be published in advance.

The *R&A* recommends:

Match Play

A match that ends all square should be played off hole by hole until one *side* wins a hole. The play-off should start on the hole where the match began. In a handicap match, handicap strokes should be allowed as in the *stipulated round*.

Stroke Play

(**a**) In the event of a tie in a scratch stroke play competition, a play-off is recommended. The play-off may be over 18 holes or a smaller number of holes as specified by the *Committee*. If that is not feasible or there is still a tie, a hole-by-hole play-off is recommended.

(**b**) In the event of a tie in a handicap stroke play competition, a play-off with handicaps is recommended. The play-off may be over 18 holes or a smaller number of holes as specified by the *Committee*. It is recommended that any such playoff consist of at least three holes.

In competitions where the handicap stroke allocation table is not relevant, if the play-off is less than 18 holes, the percentage of 18 holes played should be applied to the players' handicaps to determine their play-off handicaps. Handicap stroke fractions of one-half stroke or more should count as a full stroke and any lesser fractions should be disregarded.

In competitions where the handicap stroke table is relevant, such as four-ball stroke play and bogey, par and Stableford competitions, handicap strokes should be taken as they were assigned for the competition using the players' respective stroke allocation table(s).

(**c**) If a play-off of any type is not feasible, matching score cards is recommended. The method of matching cards should be announced in advance and should also provide what will happen if this procedure does not produce a winner. An acceptable method of matching cards is to determine the winner on the basis of the best score for the last nine holes. If the tying players have the same score for the last nine, determine the winner on the basis of the last six holes, last three holes and finally the 18th hole. If this method is used in a competition with a multiple tee start, it is recommended that the "last nine holes, last six holes, etc." is considered to be holes 10-18, 13-18, etc.

For competitions where the handicap stroke table is not relevant, such as individual stroke play, if the last nine, last six, last three holes scenario is used, one-half, one-third, one-sixth, etc. of the handicaps should be deducted from the score for those holes. In terms of the use of fractions in such deductions, the *Committee* should act in accordance with the recommendations of the relevant handicapping authority.

In competitions where the handicap stroke table is relevant, such as *four-ball* stroke play and bogey, par and Stableford competitions, handicap strokes should be taken as they were assigned for the competition, using the players' respective stroke allocation table(s).

12 Draw for Match Play

Although the draw for match play may be completely blind or certain players may be distributed through different quarters or eighths, the General Numerical Draw (see page 184) is recommended if matches are determined by a qualifying round.

General Numerical Draw

For purposes of determining places in the draw, ties in qualifying rounds other than those for the last qualifying place are decided by the order in which scores are returned, with the first score to be returned receiving the lowest available number, etc. If it is impossible to determine the order in which scores are returned, ties are determined by a blind draw.

APPENDIX I Incident

Michelle Wie (seeded second) and Maru Martinez (seeded 63rd) were playing in the first round of match play at the 2003 US Women's Amateur at Philadelphia Country Club when Martinez made a quick stop in the clubhouse, after completing the 9th hole. She was two up at the time. Martinez then received a ride from a club volunteer from the clubhouse to the 10th tee.

However, the USGA had adopted a condition that players shall walk at all times during a

UPPER HALF	LOWER HALF	UPPER HALF	LOWER HALF
64 qualifiers		**32 qualifiers**	
1 vs. 64	2 vs. 63	1 vs. 32	2 vs. 31
32 vs. 33	31 vs. 34	16 vs. 17	15 vs. 18
16 vs. 49	15 vs. 50	8 vs. 25	7 vs. 26
17 vs. 48	18 vs. 47	9 vs. 24	10 vs. 23
8 vs. 57	7 vs. 58	4 vs. 29	3 vs. 30
25 vs. 40	26 vs. 39	13 vs. 20	14 vs. 19
9 vs. 56	10 vs. 55	5 vs. 28	6 vs. 27
24 vs. 41	23 vs. 42	12 vs. 21	11 vs. 22
4 vs. 61	3 vs. 62	**16 qualifiers**	
29 vs. 36	30 vs. 35	1 vs. 16	2 vs.15
13 vs. 52	14 vs. 51	8 vs. 9	7 vs.10
20 vs. 45	19 vs. 46	4 vs. 13	3 vs.14
5 vs. 60	6 vs. 59	5 vs. 12	6 vs.11
28 vs. 37	27 vs. 38	**8 qualifiers**	
12 vs. 53	11 vs. 54	1 vs. 8	2 vs. 7
21 vs. 44	22 vs. 43	4 vs. 5	3 vs. 6

stipulated round, and it was at that point that confusion set in about how the penalty should be applied. The initial ruling had Martinez incurring a loss of hole penalty, so the players picked up from the 10th fairway and started walking to the next tee. However, before the players reached the tee, the officials came over the radio to state that the penalty was actually an adjustment to the state of the match. Therefore, the players returned to the drive zone where their tee-shots came to rest, then continued play of the hole. Wie won the 10th hole with a conceded birdie, and with the state of the match adjustment the match was now all square. Martinez commented, "I was very mad but I just said I've got to start all over again. It was my responsibility." She went on to win the match one up.

FAQ

Q How is a tie in stroke play decided?
A It is up to the Committee to determine how ties are to be decided, and the Committee should announce the procedure in advance. The R&A recommendation can be found in Appendix I, Part C, 11.

APPENDICES II AND III

The *R&A* reserves the right, at any time, to change the Rules relating to clubs and balls and make or change the interpretations relating to these Rules. For up to date information, please contact the *R&A* or refer to: www.randa.org/equipmentrules.

Any design in a club or ball which is not covered by the *Rules*, which is contrary to the purpose and intent of the *Rules*, or which might significantly change the nature of the game, will be ruled on by the *R&A*. The dimensions and limits contained in Appendices II and III are given in the units by which conformance is determined. An equivalent imperial/metric conversion is also referenced for information, calculated using a conversion rate of 1 inch = 25.4 mm.

APPENDIX II
Design of clubs

A player in doubt as to the conformity of a club should consult the *R&A*. A manufacturer should submit to the *R&A* a sample of a club to be manufactured for a ruling as to whether the club conforms with the *Rules*. The sample becomes the property of the *R&A* for reference purposes. If a manufacturer fails to submit a sample or, having submitted a sample, fails to await a ruling before manufacturing and/or marketing the club, the manufacturer assumes the risk of a ruling that the club does not conform with the *Rules*.

The following paragraphs prescribe general regulations for the design of clubs, together with specifications and interpretations. Further information relating to these regulations and their proper interpretation is provided in "A Guide to the Rules on Clubs and Balls".

Where a club, or part of a club, is required to meet a specification within the *Rules*, it must be designed and manufactured with the intention of meeting that specification.

1 Clubs
a General
A club is an implement designed to be used for striking the ball and generally comes in three forms: woods, irons and putters distinguished by shape and intended use. A putter is a club with a loft not exceeding ten degrees designed primarily for use on the *putting green*.

The club must not be substantially different from the traditional and customary form and make. The club must be composed of a shaft and a head and it may also have material added to the shaft to enable the player to obtain a firm hold (see 3 below). All parts of the club must be fixed so that the club is one unit, and it must have no external attachments. Exceptions may be made for attachments that do not affect the performance of the club.

b Adjustability
All clubs may incorporate mechanisms for weight adjustment. Other forms of adjustability may also be permitted upon evaluation by the *R&A*. The following requirements apply to all permissible methods of adjustment:
(i) the adjustment cannot be readily made;
(ii) all adjustable parts are firmly fixed and there is no reasonable likelihood of them working loose during a round; and
(iii) all configurations of adjustment conform with the *Rules*.

During a *stipulated round*, the playing characteristics of a club must not be purposely changed by adjustment or by any other means (see Rule 4-2a).

c Length
The overall length of the club must be at least 18 inches (0.457 m) and, except for putters, must not exceed 48 inches (1.219 m). For irons and woods, the measurement of length is taken when the club is lying on a horizontal plane and the sole is set against a 60 degree plane as shown in Fig. I. The length is defined as the distance from the point of the intersection between the two planes to the top of the grip. For putters, the measurement of length is taken from the top of the grip along the axis of the shaft or a straight line extension of it to the sole of the club.

d Alignment
When the club is in its normal address position the shaft must be so aligned that:
(i) the projection of the straight part of the shaft on to the vertical plane through the toe and heel must diverge from the vertical by at

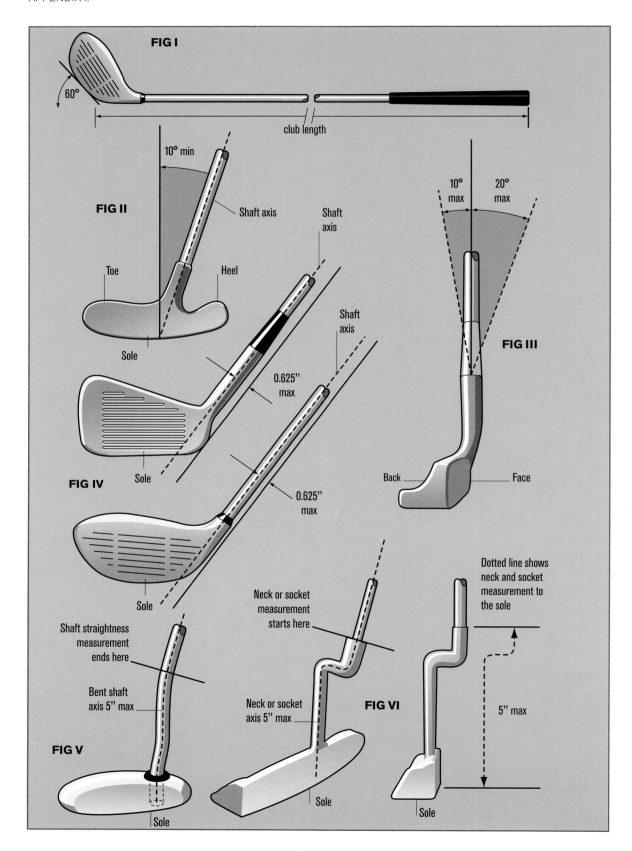

FIG I

60°

club length

FIG II

10° min

Shaft axis

Toe

Heel

Sole

Shaft axis

0.625" max

Shaft axis

FIG III

10° max

20° max

Back

Face

FIG IV

Sole

0.625" max

Sole

Shaft straightness measurement ends here

Bent shaft axis 5" max

FIG V

Sole

Neck or socket measurement starts here

Neck or socket axis 5" max

FIG VI

Sole

Dotted line shows neck and socket measurement to the sole

5" max

Sole

least 10 degrees (see Fig. II). If the overall design of the club is such that the player can effectively use the club in a vertical or close-to-vertical position, the shaft may be required to diverge from the vertical in this plane as much as 25 degrees.

(ii) the projection of the straight part of the shaft on to the vertical plane along the intended *line of play* must not diverge from the vertical by more than 20 degrees forwards or 10 degrees backwards (see Fig. III).

Except for putters, all of the heel portion of the club must lie within 0.625 inches (15.88 mm) of the plane containing the axis of the straight part of the shaft and the intended (horizontal) *line of play* (see Fig. IV).

2 Shaft

a Straightness

The shaft must be straight from the top of the grip to a point not more than 5 inches (127 mm) above the sole, measured from the point where the shaft ceases to be straight along the axis of the bent part of the shaft and the neck and/or socket (see Fig. V).

b Bending and Twisting Properties

At any point along its length, the shaft must:
(i) bend in such a way that the deflection is the same regardless of how the shaft is rotated about its longitudinal axis; and
(ii) twist the same amount in both directions.

c Attachment to Clubhead

The shaft must be attached to the clubhead at the heel either directly or through a single plain neck and/or socket. The length from the top of the neck and/or socket to the sole of the club must not exceed 5 inches (127 mm), measured along the axis of, and following any bend in, the neck and/or socket (see Fig. VI).
Exception for Putters: The shaft or neck or socket of a putter may be fixed at any point in the head.

3 Grip (see Fig. VII)

The grip consists of material added to the shaft to enable the player to obtain a firm hold. The grip must be fixed to the shaft, must be straight and plain in form, must extend to the end of the shaft and must not be moulded for any part of the hands. If no material is added, that portion of the shaft designed to be held by the player must be considered the grip.
(i) For clubs other than putters the grip must be circular in cross-section, except that a continuous, straight, slightly raised rib may be incorporated along the full length of the grip, and a slightly indented spiral is permitted on a wrapped grip or a replica of one.
(ii) A putter grip may have a non-circular cross-section, provided the cross-section has no concavity, is symmetrical and remains generally similar throughout the length of the grip. (See Clause (v) below).
(iii) The grip may be tapered but must not have any bulge or waist. Its cross-sectional dimensions measured in any direction must not exceed 1.75 inches (44.45 mm).
(iv) For clubs other than putters the axis of the grip must coincide with the axis of the shaft.
(v) A putter may have two grips provided each is circular in cross-section, the axis of each coincides with the axis of the shaft, and they are separated by at least 1.5 inches (38.1 mm).

4 Clubhead

a Plain in Shape

The clubhead must be generally plain in shape. All parts must be rigid, structural in nature and functional. The clubhead or its parts must not be designed to resemble any other object. It is not practicable to define plain in shape precisely and comprehensively. However, features that are deemed to be in breach of this requirement and are therefore not permitted include, but are not limited to:
(i) **All Clubs**
• holes through the face;
• holes through the head (some exceptions may

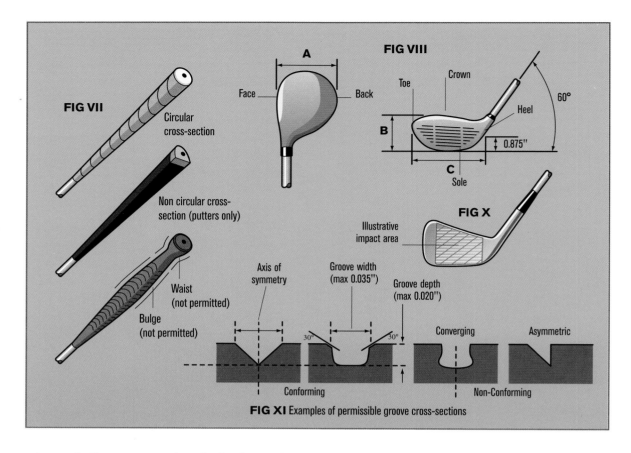

FIG VII — Circular cross-section; Non circular cross-section (putters only); Waist (not permitted); Bulge (not permitted)

FIG VIII — A; Face; Back; Toe; Crown; Heel; 60°; 0.875"; B; C; Sole

FIG X — Illustrative impact area

Axis of symmetry; Groove width (max 0.035"); Groove depth (max 0.020"); 30°; 30°; Conforming; Converging; Non-Conforming; Asymmetric

FIG XI Examples of permissible groove cross-sections

be made for putters and cavity back irons);
- features that are for the purpose of meeting dimensional specifications;
- features that extend into or ahead of the face;
- features that extend significantly above the top line of the head;
- furrows in or runners on the head that extend into the face (some exceptions may be made for putters); and
- optical or electronic devices.

(ii) Woods and Irons
- all features listed in (i) above;
- cavities in the outline of the heel and/or the toe of the head that can be viewed from above;
- severe or multiple cavities in the outline of the back of the head that can be viewed from above;
- transparent material added to the head with the intention of rendering conforming a feature that is not otherwise permitted; and

- features that extend beyond the outline of the head when viewed from above.

b Dimensions, Volume and Moment of Inertia
(i) Woods
When the club is in a 60 degree lie angle, the dimensions of the clubhead must be such that:
- the distance from the heel to the toe of the clubhead is greater than the distance from the face to the back;
- the distance from the heel to the toe of the clubhead is not greater than 5 inches (127 mm); and
- the distance from the sole to the crown of the clubhead, including any permitted features, is not greater than 2.8 inches (71.12 mm).

These dimensions are measured on horizontal lines between vertical projections of the outermost points of:
- the heel and the toe; and

- the face and the back (see Fig. VIII, dimension A);

and on vertical lines between the horizontal projections of the outermost points of the sole and the crown (see Fig. VIII, dimension B). If the outermost point of the heel is not clearly defined, it is deemed to be 0.875 inches (22.23 mm) above the horizontal plane on which the club is lying (see Fig. VIII, dimension C).

The volume of the clubhead must not exceed 460 cubic centimetres (28.06 cubic inches), plus a tolerance of 10 cubic centimetres (0.61 cubic inches).

When the club is in a 60 degree lie angle, the moment of inertia component around the vertical axis through the clubhead's centre of gravity must not exceed 5900 g cm² (32.259 oz in²), plus a test tolerance of 100 g cm² (0.547 oz in²).

(ii) Irons
When the clubhead is in its normal address position, the dimensions of the head must be such that the distance from the heel to the toe is greater than the distance from the face to the back.

(iii) Putters (see Fig. IX)
When the clubhead is in its normal address postion, the dimensions of the head much be such that:

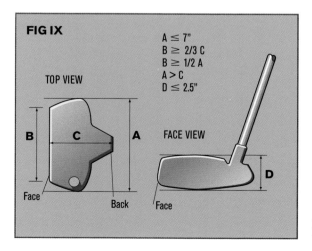

FIG IX

$A \leq 7"$
$B \geq 2/3\ C$
$B \geq 1/2\ A$
$A > C$
$D \leq 2.5"$

TOP VIEW

B   C   A

Face   Back

FACE VIEW

D

Face

- the distance from the heel to the toe is greater than the distance from the face to the back;
- the distance from the heel to the toe of the head is less than or equal to 7 inches (177.8 mm);
- the distance from the heel to the toe of the face is greater than or equal to two thirds of the distance from the face to the back of the head;
- the distance from the heel to the toe of the face is greater than or equal to half of the distance from the heel to the toe of the head; and
- the distance from the sole to the top of the head, including any permitted features, is less than or equal to 2.5 inches (63.5 mm).

For traditionally shaped heads, these dimensions will be measured on horizontal lines between vertical projections of the outermost point of:
- the heel and the toe of the head;
- the heel and the toe of the face; and
- the face and the back;

and on vertical lines between the horizontal projections of the outermost points of the sole and the top of the head.

For unusually shaped heads, the toe to heel dimension may be made at the face.

c. Spring Effect and Dynamic Properties
The design, material and/or construction of, or any treatment to, the clubhead (which includes the club face) must not:
(i) have the effect of a spring which exceeds the limit set forth in the Pendulum Test Protocol on file with the *R&A*; or
(ii) incorporate features or technology including, but not limited to, separate springs or spring features, that have the intent of, or the effect of, unduly influencing the clubhead's spring effect; or
(iii) unduly influence the movement of the ball.

Note: (i) above does not apply to putters.

d. Striking Faces

The clubhead must have only one striking face, except that a putter may have two such faces if their characteristics are the same, and they are opposite each other.

5 Club Face

a General

The face of the club must be hard and rigid and must not impart significantly more or less spin to the ball than a standard steel face (some exceptions may be made for putters). Except for such markings listed below, the club face must be smooth and must not have any degree of concavity.

b Impact Area Roughness and Material

Except for markings specified in the following paragraphs, the surface roughness within the area where impact is intended (the "impact area") must not exceed that of decorative sandblasting, or of fine milling (see Fig. X).

The whole of the impact area must be of the same material (exceptions may be made for clubheads made of wood).

c Impact Area Markings

If a club has grooves and/or punch marks in the impact area, they must be designed to meet the following specifications:

(i) Grooves

- Grooves must not have sharp edges or raised lips (test on file).
- Grooves must be straight and parallel.
- Grooves must have a symmetrical cross-section and have sides which do not converge (see Fig. XI).
- The width, spacing and cross-section of the grooves must be consistent throughout the impact area.
- Any rounding of groove edges must be in the form of a radius which does not exceed 0.020 inches (0.508 mm).
- The width of each groove must not exceed 0.035 inches (0.9 mm), using the 30 degree method of measurement on file with the *R&A*.
- The distance between edges of adjacent grooves must not be less than three times the width of the grooves, and not less than 0.075 inches (1.905 mm).
- The depth of each groove must not exceed 0.020 inches (0.508 mm).

(ii) Punch Marks

- The area of any punch mark must not exceed 0.0044 square inches (2.84 sq mm).
- The distance between adjacent punch marks (or between punch marks and grooves) must not be less than 0.168 inches (4.27 mm), measured from centre to centre.
- The depth of any punch mark must not exceed 0.040 inches (1.02 mm).
- Punch marks must not have sharp edges or raised lips (test on file).

d Decorative Markings

The centre of the impact area may be indicated by a design within the boundary of a square whose sides are 0.375 inches (9.53 mm) in length. Such a design must not unduly influence the movement of the ball. Decorative markings are permitted outside the impact area.

e Non-Metallic Club Face Markings

The above specifications do not apply to clubheads made of wood on which the impact area of the face is of a material of hardness less than the hardness of metal and whose loft angle is 24 degrees or less, but markings which could unduly influence the movement of the ball are prohibited.

f Putter Face Markings

Any markings on the face of a putter must not have sharp edges or raised lips. The specifications with regard to roughness, material and markings in the impact area do not apply.

FAQ

Q Are there any limits on club length?

A Yes. The overall length of the club shall be at least 0.457 m (18 inches) and, except for putters, must not exceed 1.219 m (48 inches).

Q Can a "chipper" have two striking faces?

A No. The Rules relating to iron clubs, and not putters, apply to the design of chippers. Decision 4-1/3 provides that:

A "chipper" is an iron club designed primarily for use off the putting green, generally with a loft greater than ten degrees. As most players adopt a "putting stroke" when using a chipper, there can be a tendency to design the club as if it was a putter. To eliminate confusion, the Rules which apply to "chippers" include:

[1] The shaft must be attached to the clubhead at the heel (Appendix II, 2c);

[2] The grip must be circular in cross-section (Appendix II, 3(i)) and only one grip is permitted (Appendix II, 3(v));

[3] The clubhead must be generally plain in shape (Appendix II, 4a) and have only one striking face (Appendix II, 4d); and

[4] The face of the club must conform to specifications with regard to hardness, surface roughness, material and markings in the impact area (Appendix II, 5).

Q Can a long putter have an adjustable shaft for travel purposes?

A Yes. However, the adjustment mechanism must be such that "adjustment cannot be readily made" (Appendix II, 1b). A screw-together ("pool-cue") joint is permitted if used in conjunction with an Allen Key screw (or similar) which penetrates the joint.

Q What are the Rules relating to the "spring" effect of driving clubs?

A The R&A's interpretation of "spring" effect in driving clubs is a measure of clubhead flexibility (or Characteristic Time). This is measured using the Pendulum Test, which consists of a steel mass suspended on a pendulum being released from varying heights to strike the clubface. The amount of time these two objects are in contact is the basis for the test, and the conformance limit has been set at 239 microseconds, plus a test tolerance of 18 microseconds.

A list of Conforming Driver Heads and the List of Non-conforming Driving Clubs (for 2008) are published on The R&A's website (www.randa.org). Further details on the situation regarding driving clubs is available on The R&A's website, including information on the Driving Club Condition of Competition and a copy of the full test protocol.

The rules, specifications and interpretations relating to clubs and balls can be found on The R&A's website or in The R&A's publication A Guide to the Rules on Clubs and Balls available from The R&A.

Q How do I find out if an item of golfing equipment I have designed conforms to the Rules or not?

A The R&A can only render a formal ruling on an item of golfing equipment if a sample is submitted for examination. However, informal opinions, based on a description, diagrams and/or photographs can sometimes be given. The R&A strongly recommends that new design ideas should be communicated or submitted as early as possible in the development process and certainly prior to beginning production of any golf club, device or component. Even though a final ruling cannot be made without the benefit of a sample, costly errors can be prevented if communication with The R&A is made as soon as possible. If a manufacturer fails to submit a sample or begins manufacturing and/or marketing an item of equipment prior to receiving an R&A ruling, the manufacturer assumes the risk of a possible ruling that the item of equipment does not conform with the Rules. Equipment submissions or enquiries should be directed to:
Equipment Standards
The R&A, St Andrews, Fife, KY16 9JD, Scotland

APPENDIX III
The ball

1 General
The ball must not be substantially different from the traditional and customary form and make. The material and construction of the ball must not be contrary to the purpose and intent of the *Rules*.

2 Weight
The weight of the ball must not be greater than 1.620 ounces avoirdupois (45.93 g).

3 Size
The diameter of the ball must not be less than 1.680 inches (42.67 mm). This specification will be satisfied if, under its own weight, a ball falls through a 1.680 inches diameter ring gauge in fewer than 25 out of 100 randomly selected positions, the test being carried out at a temperature of 23 +/-1°C.

4 Spherical Symmetry
The ball must not be designed, manufactured or intentionally modified to have properties which differ from those of a spherically symmetrical ball.

5 Initial Velocity
The initial velocity of the ball must not exceed the limit specified (test on file) when measured on apparatus approved by the *R&A*.

6 Overall Distance Standard
The combined carry and roll of the ball, when tested on apparatus approved by the *R&A*, must not exceed the distance specified under the conditions set forth in the Overall Distance Standard for golf balls on file with the *R&A*.

HANDICAPS
The Rules of Golf do not legislate for the allocation and adjustment of handicaps. Such matters are within the jurisdiction of the National Union concerned and queries should be directed accordingly.

ACKNOWLEDGEMENTS

Photographic acknowledgements:

Action Plus/Glyn Kirk 176. **Allsport** 126 left; /David Cannon 113, 144; /Stephen Dunn 63, 70; /David Frost 120; /Craig Jones 114; /Stephen Munday 16 top. **Getty Images** 19, 85, 100, 123, 164; /David Cannon 60, 72 top, 80, 145; /Stuart Franklin 15 top; /Jeff Gross 99; /Jeff Haynes 154; /Richard Heathcote 42, 45, 102, 124; /Ross Kinnaird 95; /Warren Little 138, 167; /Andy Lyons 15 bottom right, 72 bottom; /Donald Miralle 11, 37; /Andrew Redington 21, 37, 51, 66, 74, 133. **Michael G. Leemhuis** 161. **PA Photos**/Nam Y. Huh 94; /Rebecca Naden 71. **Peter Dazeley** 126 right. **Phil Sheldon Golf Picture Library** 35, 134, 178.

Illustration by Sudden Impact Media

An Hachette Livre UK Company
www.hachettelivre.co.uk

First published in Great Britain in 2003

This revised and updated edition published in 2008 by Hamlyn a division of Octopus Publishing Group Ltd
2–4 Heron Quays, London E14 4JP
www.octopusbooks.co.uk

Text copyright © R&A Rules Limited 2003, 2005, 2008
Design copyright © Octopus Publishing Group Ltd 2003, 2005, 2008

ISBN: 978-0-600-61721-1

A CIP catalogue record of this book is available from the British Library.

Printed and bound in China

10 9 8 7 6 5 4 3